ALL I WANT IS A JOB!

ALL I WANT IS A JOB!

Unemployed Women Navigating
the Public Workforce System

MARY GATTA

STANFORD ECONOMICS AND FINANCE
An Imprint of Stanford University Press
Stanford, California

Stanford University Press
Stanford, California

Special discounts for bulk quantities of titles in the Stanford Economics and Finance imprint are available to corporations, professional associations, and other organizations. For details and discount information, contact the special sales department of Stanford University Press. Tel: (650) 736-1782, Fax: (650) 736-1784

Printed in the United States of America on acid-free, archival-quality paper

Library of Congress Cataloging-in-Publication Data

Gatta, Mary Lizabeth, 1972- author.
  All I want is a job! : unemployed women navigating the public workforce system / Mary Gatta.
    pages cm
  Includes bibliographical references and index.
  ISBN 978-0-8047-8133-6 (cloth : alk. paper) —
  ISBN 978-0-8047-9082-6 (pbk. : alk. paper)
  1. Unemployed women workers—Services for—United States. 2. Women—Employment—United States. 3. Occupational training for women—United States. 4. Manpower policy—United States. I. Title.
  HD6095.G38 2014
  331.4'1370973—dc23
                                    2013047793

ISBN 978-0-8047-9085-7 (electronic)

Typeset by Bruce Lundquist in 10.5/15 Adobe Garamond

This book is dedicated to two special women:
My mother—Maria Gatta—a wonderful role model
who dedicated her life to public and volunteer
service during her short time on earth
Her business partner and friend—Dee Frankel—who continues
to share my mother's values and spirit with me every day
Cheers to you both!

Contents

Preface

This book emerged from my deep wish to better understand how women were faring as they navigated the workforce development system during the recent economic recession. Researching women's experiences in the workforce development system is not new to me. I had studied the New Jersey workforce system in the early 2000s as part of an evaluation of an innovative state Department of Labor and Workforce Development pilot program that gave the state workforce development system the latitude to implement a technology-enabled online learning program that provided education and training to a group that often did not receive it via the workforce system—working single mothers who were employed but not economically secure. The women in this program received computers, Internet access, and courses for a year to attain the education and skills to help them advance in the workplace. This project and research was very exciting to me in that it took a group of marginalized workers and helped them gain skills, certificates, and degrees in ways that were flexible and could be delivered in their homes. They were able to schedule their classes around their work and family responsibilities in an asynchronous learning environment. And the program did not just include access to education. The women also were placed with mentors and received individualized career counseling. Many of the women in the program saw a wage increase, completed their education, and gained self-confidence. They left the program excited about their ability to support themselves and their families and better assured they were on the road to economic security.[1]

However, less than ten years later that same workforce development system, similar to workforce development systems throughout the country, was under intense pressure to meet the growing numbers of unemployed men and women that resulted from the recession. I began to think again about the women I had studied earlier in the decade, and the millions more like them who were trying to navigate the system. Were they struggling? Were they experiencing unemployment and back in the public system? I had a conversation with Patricia (Pat) Leahey, a Workforce Investment Board (WIB) coordinator in New Jersey, about my desire to explore the experiences women had in the workforce system, and she granted me access to conduct focus groups and interviews[2] with clients and helped arrange these for me in her local area. That first day of focus groups was sobering. Women shared their stories—how they got to be unemployed, what their hopes for the future were, and what it was like to be a client in the system. Some of what we learned was positive and encouraging; much of it was disturbing.

After I completed a first set of focus groups, Pat and I debriefed at our favorite coffee house on the Jersey Shore. She wanted to delve deeper into the stories that the women shared with us in the focus groups about what was working and what was not working. We heard about different stumbling blocks from the women we spoke to and how staff did (or did not) work with them to provide career guidance and planning. Pat wanted to try to better figure out what was occurring in the field with the purpose of trying to improve service delivery. She also saw what I was learning via the focus groups and interviews as part of larger evaluations the One Stop Career Centers—both locally and throughout the state—were engaging in to try to improve service. I suggested that I should go "undercover" as a client to try find out more. Instead of laughing off my sociological interest or running away from it for fear of what she would learn, Pat embraced the idea. She got approvals from her colleagues, and we put a plan together to do the undercover research.[3] She was clear that she wanted me to do this to try to address some of the concerns that the female clients reported to us in focus groups, not to expose her local area or individual workers.

So we set ground rules and got to work. For instance, at no point in my undercover work would I take a spot from a client. Instead, I would only use services in which I could be an "extra." This meant I would not meet one on one with a staff member (unless I spoke with a staff member after or before a workshop I attended) but instead would focus on core services and the One Stop Career Center's classes and workshops. I would also not expose any workers by name. In fact, all of my notes would have no identifying information on the staff. I was focused on process and substance, not on checking up on particular staff members. After the participant observation I would again conduct focus groups and interviews with additional clients and also with the front-line workers. Looping back with qualitative research after my participant observation not only allowed me the opportunity to increase my credibility among the clients and staff I would interview, but also allowed for a richer and more comprehensive discussion with my new-found firsthand knowledge.

This book is the product of that research. It is not meant to be an exposé of the workforce system in which I went undercover. Instead I focused on delving deeply into the processes of the workforce system; identifying effective existing practices, along with areas in which challenges existed; and uncovering the clients' and front-line workers' standpoints and their perspectives on the workforce system. Indeed, there were several things that were working well. And when things were not working well, both the local area and the state Department of Labor and Workforce Development were eager to learn about those items and try to work to improve them.

In the pages that follow I attempt to represent the incredible opportunity I had to probe the workforce system at a time when it was facing immense pressures—when unemployment was very high, the system was pushed to its maximum, and individuals' economic anxiety was profound. It is my hope that it helps to put a face on the workforce system—both for the client and the staff—so that we can continue to better understand a system that is needed in both good and bad economic times.

Acknowledgments

All books are true collaborations, and this one is no exception. This book truly benefited from the intellectual insights and support of many individuals.

I want to thank Patricia Leahey, Michelle Hutchinson, and Maria Gonzalez, leaders of the Ocean County workforce system where I conducted my study. They are among the most dedicated women I have had the pleasure of working with, and demonstrated an unfailing commitment to this project. They provided me with access to their facilities and programs, and were always willing to provide information and data for the project. Special mention must be made of Dianne Mills McKay and the New Jersey Council on Gender Parity in Labor and Education. Dianne saw the promise in this project from the beginning and continues to help to ensure that women's needs are met in New Jersey. I also want to thank the many clients and front-line workers who gave of their time and their stories to sit down with me to share their experiences. Their time, honesty, and commitment made this book possible.

Throughout the course of writing this book, I was fortunate to benefit from two sets of amazing colleagues and intellectual environments. When I began this project I was working at the Center for Women and Work at Rutgers University, a place that very much grounded my intellectual thinking. In 2010 I joined Wider Opportunities for Women (WOW). It is through my work and support from my colleagues at WOW that this book took its shape and blossomed.

I am grateful for the assistance and support of the editorial staff at Stanford University Press. Margo Fleming is the most wonderful and thoughtful editor one can ask for. She saw the promise in this book, provided immediate feedback at every step of this project, offered un-flagging encouragement, and pushed me to make this book all it could be. I am also grateful to the detailed review of this manuscript by Henry Plotkin, Ofer Sharone, and an anonymous reviewer. All three provided not only critical perspective but also invaluable suggestions that really moved this from a draft manuscript to a book.

Finally, a special note to my husband, Mike Glory, for his support in the years it took to put this book together. Looking forward to a cel-ebratory drink with you!

ALL I WANT IS A JOB!

Introduction

I nervously entered the building and immediately was greeted by a large sign that read "STOP! EVERYONE MUST CHECK IN AT THE COUNTER." I waited in a line behind three people, and when it became my turn I sheepishly told the receptionist, "I am here for the reemployment seminar." Without even looking at me, she said, "Straight back to room 104." I entered the room, where I saw at least twenty-five adults sitting classroom style in silence, nervously trying to avoid eye contact with each other.

Finally the instructor entered the room. He greeted us by saying, "Welcome to the reemployment seminar; you are all required to be in this seminar because the unemployment office thinks you will have a really hard time finding a job in this economy."

.   .   .

This experience marked the beginning of my six-month journey going undercover at a public One Stop Career Center[1] during one of the deepest recessions in modern history. In December of 2007, the United States entered an acute stage of economic distress. Unemployment reached levels that had not been seen in decades, and the underemployment of workers increased at record rates. From December 2007 to early 2010 the nation lost 8.7 million jobs and left fifteen million workers unemployed. And an overwhelming majority of Americans—73 percent—either knew someone who lost his or her job or were themselves among those fifteen million workers trying to survive unemployment during the recession.[2] The unemployed can learn quickly that the One Stop Career Center is intended to be their first stop on their way to reemployment. Mandated by the federal Workforce Investment Act (WIA), One Stops house a collection of employment and training services—including programs that are part of the Wagner-Peyser Act, vocational rehabilitation, and assistance for veteran's affairs. One Stop Career Centers are currently the centerpiece in this country's workforce development policy and were ground zero in the response to the economic recession. The U.S. Department of Labor reports that there are 1,757 comprehensive One Stop Career Centers and 988 affiliate centers throughout the country.[3] So slightly fewer than 2,750 One Stop Career Centers make up the front lines of the nation's workforce development system. Yet while occasionally a photograph would appear in the *New York Times* or another media outlet that showed unemployed workers in the One Stop Career Centers looking for jobs and using the available services, there surprisingly has been little attention or deep inquiry into these centers during the recession.

As the economic crisis wore on, I would listen to members of Congress, various state governors, and even the president talk about the nation's policy response to the massive unemployment in the recession—suggesting what was working and what was not working. Yet they never really posed some of the questions that nagged at me during this recession. What was it like to be among the millions of unemployed workers who entered the One Stop Career Centers during the recession? Or to be one of the thousands who worked in the field each day? What activities actually went on in those centers? Were individuals being matched to available jobs? Did these jobs provide economic security for those individuals and their families? And did economic security even matter in the field, or is it really just about job placement? I could not help but wonder if the people who were located on the front lines of the recession—the many unemployed, along with the workers staffing the One Stop Career Centers—had insight to inform the nation's employment and training policy. As an ethnographic sociologist, I set out to investigate and chronicle the experiences of unemployed workers, and in particular unemployed women, as they used public workforce services and struggled to survive unemployment.

What drew me to this work is that very little is known about One Stop Career Centers and workforce development policy from a critical policy standpoint.[4] The WIA, like many social policies, is typically evaluated with quantitative performance measures. For instance, the number of clients served at different levels of service (although some states do not break down the levels of service within demographic categories[5]) is known, as are the number of people placed in jobs, the number of those placed in training programs, and the number of those referred to other services.[6] What is not known, and often may not even be questioned, are more qualitative assessments of success such as, "Did the right person get the right training or education?" "How were clients treated?" or "Were women placed in nontraditional jobs?"[7] In addition, there is a bit of "sloppiness" around workforce policy in some circles. For instance, it is sometimes assumed to be synonymous with welfare policy, on the basis of an incorrect assumption that all the clients served in the One Stop Career Centers are similar in characteristics to those served by welfare. And misconceptions about these centers are themselves quite abundant. Many assume that the One Stop Career Centers are simply the unemployment offices—a place where one goes only to complete their forms to apply for unemployment insurance or troubleshoot why their unemployment check was not processed. And for some Americans, the One Stop Career Centers are not often on their radar screens; they simply do not know they exist!

My goal is to explore and critically evaluate the lived experiences of the individuals, and in particular women, who are served by and working in the One Stop Career Centers, in order to challenge mainstream understandings of workforce development policy. In doing so, I engage a framework that is intended to uncover and highlight the lived experiences of the individuals who are standing on the ground floor. I ask questions such as the following:

1. How is policy implemented and practiced in One Stop Career Centers at the local level?

2. What are the lived experiences of clients, and specifically female clients, along with the workers serving them? How are women served in the workforce system, and how is that experience gendered?

3. How can workforce policy be configured around the lives and social practices of the people most affected by that policy?

To gather the information to answer these questions, I not only conducted interviews and focus groups with unemployed workers and front-line staff but also went undercover and attempted to navigate the public workforce system as an unemployed woman. This way, I was able to delve deeply into the processes of the workforce system, to identify what practices were working well and where challenges existed. This participant observation perspective also afforded me the opportunity to share what it means and feels like to be among the clients in the workforce system. To the best of my knowledge, while "secret shopping" is sometimes used as an evaluation tool for One Stop Career Centers, such an ethnographic sociological analysis with this level of depth has never been conducted.

What Is Workforce Development?

Since the implementation of the 1998 Workforce Investment Act, the term *workforce development system* has been used ubiquitously to describe a vast and somewhat all-encompassing system. Although One Stop Career Centers—centralized organizations that co-locate public services and programs related to employment and training—have been part of the workforce system in some form for over three decades,[8] they became the primary service delivery approach in the 1990s. The piloting and eventual institutionalization of One Stop Career Centers represents a key structure of the current workforce development system, which was based on the tenet that services should be streamlined, so that all employment and training programs for all people could be brought together and be easily accessible. To accomplish this, programs and job services are grouped together into a tiered sequence of services. One Stop Career Centers include a variety of services from lower-cost core services[9] such as computerized job listings, basic labor market information, and self-service job assistance tools, along with higher-cost intensive services[10] such as individualized career counseling and training.[11]

The One Stops—in both physical and virtual formats—have become a central part of the United States's workforce development system.

One key aspect of the development of One Stop Career Centers is that they are mandated to serve all workers. This includes the unemployed and the underemployed, along with individuals from all ages, educational levels, occupations, and industries. This is often referred to as the "universal access" component of workforce development. However, this mandate, in both policy and practice, does not translate into a universality of all services for all individuals. On average, while nearly fifteen million people are served annually by One Stop Career Centers, it appears that the bulk of these workers receive core services.[12] In fact, the universal access component mandates that any individual is entitled to go into a physical One Stop Career Center, or online in a virtual format, to access core services. These resources are often geared to assist individuals in making decisions about careers to pursue available labor market information and job search tools (such as online listings). No such mandate exists for intensive or training services. Instead, eligibility thresholds—such as income, unemployment status, and multiple individual-level barriers to employment (including literacy levels, incarceration status)—serve as filters for these services. Core services then appear to have the largest number of clients accessing services, and in contrast only about 3 percent of individuals receive intensive services each year.[13] And because the end goal of workforce policy is that an individual is placed in a job, if one can be placed in a job with a revamping of a resume or access to online job postings, then WIA policy is interpreted to be understood that there would be no need for additional services.

The usage data points highlight both the policy that currently grounds the workforce development system and the tension that is embedded in that policy. Workforce development is currently a work-first system, and like any system that is directed to immediate job placement, it often exists at the expense of training and career development.[14] Workforce development has taken on the characteristics of welfare reform in many ways—in which getting an individual a job is what is needed, often with less consideration paid to the quality of that job. Today's One Stop Career Centers, and the public workforce system they are part of, have evolved out of employment policies that guided the system over the past century. These policy changes shifted from a climate in which workforce development traditionally served disadvantaged populations by providing access to short-term training and skills development to a current system that is supposed to serve multiple partners, roles, and targets.[15] However, the reality is—whether by necessity or tradition—the workforce system has maintained a particular emphasis on individuals facing obstacles in the labor market. These include men and women with prison records, along with those with little formal education, low literacy, and little work experience. These individuals often need a comprehensive approach of case management, including the time and resources to "assess [their] need and abilities; referrals to resources and supports; education and training; coaching; referrals to jobs and post-employment services."[16] Yet with the tiered sequences of services and work-first performance goals, the ability to receive such a comprehensive approach is questionable. And immediate placement in a job can become more of a weak band-aid fix—often dooming workers to a lifetime in the low-wage labor market with few opportunities for advancement.

This reality is grounded in a policy framework that insists the workforce development system is not just about workers needing services. While workers are an important focus of the workforce development system, there is also a significant role that is performed by employers. Employers are expected to serve as full partners in the WIA by identifying skill needs, codeveloping training programs, leveraging public resources, and creating a pipeline through which skilled workers can advance. Ideally, this is conceived as a symbiotic association that results in a "workforce development [that] is the coordination of school, company, and government policies and programs such that as a collective they enable individuals the opportunity to realize a sustainable livelihood and organizations to achieve exemplary goals consistent with history, culture, and goals of the societal context."[17] Given that, programs and services for employers—such as identifying and prescreening potential employees to customized training—have been a significant part of the workforce system.

On the surface such a framework makes some sense. If jobs are needed, then clearly employers must be part of the process. However, when one digs a bit deeper, some questions emerge. Is the workforce system, in ways similar to the welfare system, serving as a feeder to employers for low-wage workers? There is actually much discussion about the ways that the WIA is expected to meet the needs of employers and workers simultaneously. The rhetoric in the WIA recommends that central to creating a system that can meet the needs of workers and employers is the development of a flexible and customized system that addresses job needs and shortages, labor market changes, and the learning and skills training gaps of existing and potential workers in concert with the skills demanded by employers. This policy led the National Governor's Association to note that "in this version workforce development policies no longer address the 'second chance' system as they have in the past, but they are customized to the needs of individuals and employers."[18] To do this it seems as if the workforce development system must provide a coherent, easily accessible, and high-quality lifelong learning system. Skill demands are continually evolving, and workers need both occupationally specific and flexible skills in order to adapt and thrive. There is quite a wide pool of workers in need of these services: individuals who are looking for first-time employment; those who are currently employed full or part time but want to advance in the labor market; men and women who are undergoing transitions in their employment; individuals who were employed at one time, but are no longer currently employed (those in prison and retirees); and even workers who have been recruited from other locations for employment (such as guest workers and immigrants).[19]

And as the policy exists now, it appears that the dual customer approach of workers and employers may not be benefiting each group equally. Policy researchers Kathleen Shaw and Sara Rab noted that the training needs of employers may not be the same as those of workers. Their case study of the Florida workforce system found that employers often need short-term, non-degree-bearing training for the immediate filling of their labor needs. However, for workers, research clearly shows that they receive higher economic returns by completing degree- and certificate-bearing programs. This led Shaw and Rab to emphasize that "the student consumer is generally not well served by the existing type of programs. Instead the customer that benefits here is the business community, which in Florida's economy in particular sustains a demand for a supply of workers willing to work for low wages."[20]

A goal of full customer satisfaction in workforce development—when customers are both employers and employees—would be a true symbiotic relationship, which would require a rethinking and strong commitment to understanding what can truly benefit both groups. Employers need workers and workers need the jobs that employers provide. However, what appears to be missing in this understanding is that employers needed skilled workers at all levels, and workers need not only jobs but good-quality jobs. This requires investment in workers via skills training and education, something that requires funding and time resources. Yet, unlike with many other social service programs or income transfer programs,[21] the benefits of workforce development programs are not often immediately evidenced to either individuals or employers, but instead occur over time.

Center for Law and Social Policy researchers Neil Ridley and Elizabeth Kenefick's review of quasi-experimental evaluations of the WIA since 2000 have demonstrated that the value of training and workforce services can be evidenced in the long term. For instance, a review of adult participants in twelve states found that while individuals who completed training services had lower initial returns, they caught up to others within ten quarters, ultimately registering total gains of $800 for women and $500 to $600 for men per quarter. The researchers also note that training programs have the impact of lowering business employers' costs over time, by improving a business's ability to find and retain qualified workers and increasing the productivity and skills of existing workers. They share an example of a hospital participating in a health care initiative. Through that training program the hospital documented $40,000 in savings as a result of lower turnover and reduced hiring costs. There is increasing evidence that workforce development for adults has the ability to have an impact on the life chances of future generations.[22] Further, Ridley and Kenefick, citing University of Wisconsin social work professor Katherine Magnuson's research on adult education of mothers, suggest that when mothers with low education levels complete further education, their children appear to have improved language and reading skills.[23]

Studies such as these highlight what is currently the smallest portion of workforce development—investing in the human capital of individuals via the formal degree and certificate system. Of course, as with any investment that will pay off in the future it has an element of risk to it. The United States Conference of Mayors in 2002 equated the investment in workforce development programs to the investment that high school seniors make in college. As they note,

Students enroll in college and incur substantial costs both in terms of tuition, books, and fees as well as forgone earnings. . . . However, most of the benefits of a college education will occur after college is completed, and the earnings gains will occur over the entire work life. But like all investment activities considerable uncertainty attends the college investment decision because the expected benefits will only occur in the future well after the costs have been incurred and, for some high school graduates, college will prove to be a failed investment. . . . Nonetheless, changes in the job content of the American economy have sharply increased the economic returns to a four year college degree.[24]

This highlights a key aspect of the tension in workforce development that I was interested in exploring more—immediate job placement versus investments in human capital development. At a time with high levels of unemployment and pressure for immediate labor market attachment—from both policy performance measure standpoints and unemployed clients—investments in human capital via the workforce system are increasingly less likely. That tension of putting the unemployed back to work as opposed to investing time and resources to provide skills training that could support longer-term economic security is particularly pronounced with low-wage workers.

Investing in workforce training for low-wage workers will have economic benefits that are evidenced over their lifetime. The workers may not experience wage increases or promotions immediately upon completion of training programs, but instead may experience them a year or two after it is completed. Therefore, the framework that guides and measures the workforce development policies must be flexible enough to understand that, similar to college education, workforce training programs could be focused on enhancing the quality of the labor force and providing individuals with the human capital to improve their lives.

Yet, in a time of high unemployment and performance measurement based on placing people in jobs—regardless of whether those jobs exist or even offer economic security pathways, can such a vision materialize in practice? The quality of jobs that are available in the labor market complicates and frustrates this picture. The numbers of low-wage and low-quality jobs are growing in the United States. An important guiding notion in this book is that while the welfare and workforce development systems succeeded in mobilizing groups of workers in the early 2000s, it never provided the next step of economically secure jobs. And currently the workforce system is experiencing challenges meeting the needs of the growing number of dislocated workers in this current economic recession and recovery—an increasing number of whom may be older, professional, skilled, or educated workers who may need retraining to qualify for new jobs in the economy. Using the voices of the clients and staff, along with my own experiences undercover in the One Stop system, I explore where the situation currently stands, with the goal of better understanding workforce policy and the labor market so that the former can better meet the diverse needs of today's workforce.

These more macro-level concerns are played out in the micro daily interactions at the One Stop Career Center. For example, the tensions between immediate job placement and access to education and training led to situations in which clients were confused about what was expected and available to them. Some clients who enter the One Stop

Career Center feel they need additional training, retraining, education, or all of the above to find a new job. They often enter the orientation classes excited about the possibility that they could be able to receive training vouchers. To give just one example, at my first orientation seminar, called a "reemployment seminar," I was told that I could simply pick a job off of the state's labor market information website and then find a training provider. When I followed up on this, however, I learned I would need to go through a series of courses, eligibility requirements, and documented job search processes before I could get to a training option. And I learned that, after going through all those hurdles, even if I did qualify for training, the county itself did not have available training dollars, and there was no state funding left to pay for training either. So if I qualified, I was out of luck in terms of actually receiving the funding to attain training. Perhaps most distressing was the fact that some of my fellow clients interpreted what we learned differently than I, so they signed up for classes without noting the fine print. Those clients often ended up with nonrefundable courses, which could only be paid out of personal funds. For clients, especially low-wage clients, this is an expense that they cannot afford.

Further, my fellow clients and I were repeatedly reminded that the goal of the One Stop Career Center was to get us a job, and perhaps more aptly, get us *any* job. There was little discussion on what that new job would be or if the wages would actually provide enough income to support oneself. For all workers, and particularly low-wage workers, the focus on job placement in the One Stop system may meet the need of immediate employment, but it does not address the larger issues of earning enough income to pay the bills and be economically secure.

In addition to focusing on the challenges of low-wage clients, my research explores the challenges that workers with higher levels of education or extensive work experience faced in their use of the One Stop system. While the WIA mandate is to provide universal access, meaning that all individuals must be served, it was clear very early on that there was not a system in place to address the challenges of workers with years of experience or higher levels of education. For instance, in a job search seminar that I attended, a fellow client who had spent years as a pharmaceutical manager was instructed to go to a Michael's crafts store to apply for a job because her hobby was needlework. As another client put it,

I go into a One Stop because I can see the big sign, "Hey get a job." But I am not necessarily the person they want to reach out to, not within their heart, not emotionally. They tell me, "Oh I am sorry ma'am, you already have a degree, you are marketable. Go out there and get a job." Let's see, if I wanted a job, if I could get a job, I would go out and just get it. If I didn't want a job, I wouldn't come in here and ask you for your assistance. You can't hit the pavement, that is not how they do it. You have to get on the Internet and you fill out all of this paperwork. And I am sitting here and thinking, "Please hire me."

Of course not all clients had negative experiences. Not only can the public workforce system work to help individuals get the training that they may need to find new jobs, it also can help to build their self-confidence at one of the lowest points of their lives. One woman talked about how lost she was prior to coming into the One Stop Career Center, and how a counselor there helped to direct her:

When I went there I had randomly picked these schools, not knowing exactly what I needed and what I should be learning. They were helpful in that. Finding a program of study that included what I wanted to learn. In fact, even when I came here and met with my counselor, she changed something around for me. She thought I would be better suited where she put me.

Positive experiences like this teach us a great deal about the potential of the workforce system to meet the diversity of client needs, along with the importance of career counseling and guidance. And often in these more effective cases the workforce system is serving as a career center and not just a job placement agency.

However, sharing the experiences of the clients is only part of the story. Believing that public policy is a coproduction of both workforce clients and workforce staff, I also talked with front-line workers in the workforce system. What is it like to be a front-line worker in an employment center in this recession? Are the available resources adequate to meet the needs in the field? Among other things, these workers talked about the emotional labor they must perform as they see jobless after jobless workers come into their offices.[25]

Within the last two years, it really is emotionally draining. I have found that it is sometimes very hard to hold back tears, which I know is very unprofessional. But some of these stories are very hard to hear. These people are losing everything they have ever worked for in their entire life, and it could be any one of us at any given time. We try our best to do as much as we can and at least give them some direction from the moment they walk in so they are not floundering and saying, "Is there any hope?"

This book chronicles the experiences and needs of both the workers and the clients in the One Stop Career Center. Unemployed workers need help coping with the economic crisis—identifying where the current and new job opportunities are likely to be and how to develop the skills for them. One Stop Career Center workers need resources and professional development opportunities to better serve the clients at their door. How is the current system meeting this challenge? And how is it doing so with diminished resources? Since 1980, workforce development expenditures have fallen by as much as 90 percent, while the U.S. economy has doubled in size and its workforce has grown by nearly half.[26] The workforce system, which was already ill-equipped to deal with the massive challenges workers at all rungs of the skill ladder are facing, will require greater investment and development in a post-economic-recession world. Through my research, I dig deep into the system in order to focus on ways that challenges and barriers in the workforce system can be addressed, along with recommendations to streamline and improve that system and help unemployed Americans return to work.

The Labor Market—
What Did the Situation Look Like for Women?

I began this journey most interested in the experiences of women among the working poor in the early 2000s who then found themselves unemployed as the recession took hold. Not surprisingly, many of the women had spent years in the low-wage labor market—some considered a success by welfare reform standards—only to find them-selves many times economically worse off and in the grips of a deep national recession.

To understand the experiences of low-wage women workers, it is helpful to appreciate the structural constraints of the low-wage job market from which they emerged and to which they are likely to return. The low-wage job market, characterized by low pay, a lack of health benefits and pensions, little control over one's hours, shift work that is often outside of standard work hours, and little opportunity for ad-vancement, has been a stopping ground for single mothers and women entering work post-welfare reform. Women constitute 60 percent of the low-wage labor market, and they are employed in occupations such as retail sales, assistant positions, child care, waitressing, cashiering, fast food, bartending, home health aide, housekeeping, and package han-dling. Indeed, in the entire female labor force, close to one-third of the women workers are in the low-wage labor market (as opposed to one-fifth of men) and earn less than $25,000 annually.[27] In addition, low-wage work is difficult to escape. While there is movement in and out of low-wage jobs, two-thirds of those who moved to better-paying jobs returned to low-wage work, with women in particular exiting and then returning.[28]

Of course, women are not evenly distributed in low-wage work. Instead, gender intersects with race, ethnicity, and class to marginalize groups of women within low-wage work. While researchers have often focused on the gender division of labor in service work, this focus can mask differences among women, particularly around race and ethnicity in services. For instance, white women tend to be in service jobs that are in the "public's eye" and require the most interactions and emotional labor; women of color are over-represented in "dirty back room" jobs, such as housekeeping and kitchen work.[29]

In her ethnographic account of luxury hotel work, sociologist Rachel Sherman found similar patterns. She noted that hotel work is divided into two main categories: interactive and non-interactive. Interactive or "front of the house" work consists mainly of intangible emotional labor, while "back of the house," non-interactive work mainly involves physical labor. Sherman went on to point out that interactive workers are usually white (with the exception of bellmen and door attendants, who provide more physical work and are usually men of color), and "back of the house" workers are typically people of color and immigrants. In addition, Sherman found wage differences with each category of hotel work. Not only were back-of-the-house workers paid less than front-of-the-house workers (about one to two dollars less per hour in the sites Sherman reviewed), they also did not typically receive the tips that front-of-the-house workers received from hotel guests.[30]

So, it is not just low-wage work, it is the gendered and racialized nature of the labor market that these women (and countless others) exist in. This was highlighted in the recent economic recession as the public discourse directed attention to the impact of men in the recession. It is true that this recession, like previous recessions, hit predominantly male sectors of the economy hard. About half of the job losses during the recession were in manufacturing and transportation sectors (sectors that are about 76 percent male). Construction saw a 23.3 percent decrease in employment; manufacturing and trade experienced a 16 percent decline; and transportation and utilities industries saw a 7.6 percent decline. Another 18 percent of job losses were in administrative and waste services (which are about 60 percent male).[31] Conversely, education and health services (which are 77 percent female) saw an increase of 4.5 percent employment, and public administration and government (57 percent female) also experienced a small 0.6 percent growth.[32] The job loss in predominantly male industries led many commentators to dub this recession the "Great Mancession."

However, while job losses were higher in male-dominated industries during the recession, it did not mean that women fared well. In fact, the reality was quite to the contrary. Single women who were heads of households were almost twice as likely to be unemployed as married women or men—a rate of 12.6 percent. In contrast, the unemployment rate for all men was 10.5 percent, and for all women was 8.1 percent.

During the recession, 13 percent of women who were the sole bread-winners for their families were unemployed, compared to 7.4 percent of married men or 5.5 percent of married women.[33]

Women of color also fared poorly in the recession. During the recession, African American women's unemployment rate was at 13.4 percent, Hispanic women had an unemployment rate of 11.3 percent, while white women's rate was at 7.2 percent. Educational attainment also was a key factor in unemployment, as women with less than a high school diploma experienced the highest unemployment rate of any group, averaging 9.5 percent unemployment in the past decade, compared with 7.8 percent unemployment for men without a high school diploma and 2.6 percent unemployment for women and men with college degrees. And in a comparison among women, the average gap between those with and without a high school diploma or more (4.6 percentage points) is much larger than the gap between men with and without a high school diploma or more (2.4 percentage points).[34]

Further, even when women held onto employment in the recession, they remained concentrated in low-paying occupations. During the recession, the leading five occupations for women were (in order) secretaries, registered nurses, elementary and middle school teachers, retail salespersons, and cashiers. Women remain in traditionally female occupations, some of which do not have career ladders, economic security wages, and pensions.[35] And not only were women located in the lowest-paying occupations, they continued to earn less than their male counterparts across all occupations. During the recession, the pay gap stood at around 78 percent—with women earning 78 cents to every man's dollar. This remained true across all categories of women, and even when women invest in their education, that investment pays off differently for them relative to comparable men. The American Association of University Women reported that, one year out of college, women working full time earn only 80 percent as much as their male college-educated colleagues earn. Ten years after graduation, women fall farther behind, earning only 77 percent as much as men earn.[36] So while women experienced less unemployment relative to men during the recession, they were able to hold their jobs, in part, because they are "cheaper" labor. Women work in traditionally lower-paying jobs, often without benefits and pensions, and even when they work alongside men, they are earning less because of the pay gap.

While fewer women than men may have lost their jobs during the recession, women were clearly being left behind when the economy began to show some recovery. From 2009 onward, men found jobs in sectors where women have not, and men have made stronger advances than women in other sectors.[37] In particular, women lost a total of 433,000 jobs in manufacturing, retail trade, and finance during the recovery, while men gained 253,000 jobs in those sectors. Even in sectors in which women had made inroads prior to the recession—such as the professional and business services and education and health services—men did better than women. Specifically, even though 691,000 new jobs in those sectors went to women, men gained 804,000 jobs in those sectors. Meanwhile, not all women experienced the recovery equally. During the recovery the unemployment rate for black women grew to 14 percent and for Hispanic women that rate grew to 12.3 percent. For white women the unemployment rate stood at 6.6 percent during the recovery.[38]

A look at women's occupational distribution in the recovery demonstrates a worsening of the already precarious position women find themselves in in the labor market. Table I.1 clearly shows that women overall remain segregated in low-wage, traditionally female occupations. The majority of women workers (50.3 percent) are concentrated in 26 occupational categories, or only 5 percent of the 504 occupations tracked by the U.S. Bureau of Labor Statistics. And over two-thirds of women are concentrated in 51 occupations. The leading occupations for women remain secretaries, registered nurses, elementary and middle school teachers, retail salespersons, and cashiers. This is true pre-recession, during the recession, and in the recovery. And even in traditionally female jobs, women continue to earn less than their male counterparts.

TABLE I.1. Top fifty-one occupations employing women, and their median weekly earnings

Occupational Category	Total Number Employed (Thousands)	Percentage of Women Employed	Total Number of Women Employed (Thousands)	Cumulative Percentage of All Working Women	Men's Median Weekly Earnings*	Women's Median Weekly Earnings*
1 Secretaries and Administrative Assistants	3,082	96.1	2,963	4.5	$725	$657
2 Registered Nurses	2,843	91.1	2,590	8.5	$1,201	$1,039
3 Elementary and Middle School Teachers	2,813	81.8	2,300	12.0	$1,024	$931
4 Cashiers	3,109	73.7	2,293	15.4	$400	$366
5 Retail Salespersons	3,286	51.9	1,705	18.0	$651	$421
6 Nursing, Psychiatric, and Home Health Aides	1,928	88.2	1,700	20.6	$488	$427
7 Waiters and Waitresses	2,067	71.1	1,470	22.9	$450	$381
8 First-Line Supervisors and Managers of Retail Sales Workers	3,132	43.9	1,376	25.0	$782	$578
9 Customer Service Representatives	1,896	66.6	1,263	26.9	$614	$586
10 Maids and Housekeeping Cleaners	1,407	89.0	1,252	28.8	$455	$376
11 Receptionists and Information Clerks	1,281	92.7	1,188	30.6	$547	$529
12 Child Care Workers	1,247	94.7	1,181	32.4	**	$398
13 Bookkeeping, Accounting, and Auditing Clerks	1,297	90.9	1,179	34.2	$677	$628
ONE THIRD OF WOMEN WORKERS						
14 First-Line Supervisors and Managers of Office and Administrative Support Workers	1,507	68.7	1,035	35.8	$890	$726
15 Managers, All Other	2,898	35.0	1,013	37.3	$1,395	$1,045
16 Accountants and Auditors	1,646	60.1	989	38.8	$1,273	$953
17 Teacher Assistants	966	92.4	892	40.2	**	$485

#	Occupation						
18	Personal and Home Care Aides	973	86.1	839	41.4	$414	$405
19	Office Clerks, General	994	84.2	837	42.7	$632	$597
20	Cooks	1,951	40.5	790	43.9	$401	$381
21	Medical Assistants and Other Health Care Support Occupations	850	89.7	762	45.1	$518	$500
22	Janitors and Building Cleaners	2,186	33.2	726	46.2	$494	$400
23	Hairdressers, Hairstylists, and Cosmetologists	770	91.9	708	47.3	**	$462
24	Secondary School Teachers	1,221	57.0	696	48.3	$1,035	$962
25	Preschool and Kindergarten Teachers	712	97.0	691	49.4	**	$621
26	Social Workers	771	80.8	623	50.3	$865	$788
	ONE HALF OF WOMEN WORKERS						
27	Financial Managers	1,141	53.2	607	51.2	$1,546	$1,022
28	Post-Secondary Teachers	1,300	45.9	597	52.1	$1,308	$1,011
29	Human Resources, Training, and Labor Relations Specialists	824	70.3	579	53.0	$1,101	$874
30	Other Teachers and Instructors	806	66.5	536	53.8	$927	$714
31	Licensed Practical and Licensed Vocational Nurses	573	91.7	525	54.6	**	$716
32	Stock Clerks and Order Fillers	1,456	36.0	525	55.4	$471	$495
33	Education Administrators	830	63.0	523	56.2	$1,396	$1,137
34	Counselors	702	51.8	500	57.0	$780	$818
35	Real Estate Brokers and Sales Agents	854	54.0	461	57.7	$978	$683
36	Food Service Managers	960	47.4	455	58.4	$796	$626
37	Billing and Posting Clerks and Machine Operators	472	92.2	435	59.1	**	$607
38	Marketing and Sales Managers	959	45.2	433	59.7	$1,534	$1,010

(continued)

TABLE 1.1. *(continued)*

Occupational Category	Total Number Employed (Thousands)	Percentage of Women Employed	Total Number of Women Employed (Thousands)	Cumulative Percentage of All Working Women	Men's Median Weekly Earnings*	Women's Median Weekly Earnings*
39 Designers	793	53.7	426	60.4	$1,001	$757
40 Food Preparation Workers	717	59.2	425	61.0	$390	$367
41 Tellers	453	88.0	399	61.6	**	$490
42 Medical and Health Services Managers	549	72.5	398	62.2	1,510	$1,163
43 Office and Administrative Support Workers, All Other	501	79.0	395	62.8	750	$632
44 Chief Executives	1,505	25.5	383	63.4	$2,217	$1,598
45 Health Diagnosing and Treating Practitioner Support Technicians	505	75.9	383	64.0	$639	$606
46 Special Education Teachers	387	85.1	329	64.5	$993	$960
47 Lawyers	1,040	31.5	327	65.0	$1,895	$1,461
48 Sales Representatives, Wholesale and Manufacturing	1,284	25.0	321	65.5	$983	$842
49 First-Line Supervisors and Managers of Non-Retail Sales Workers	1,131	28.0	316	66.0	$1,035	$801
50 First-Line Supervisors and Managers of Food Preparation and Serving Workers	551	56.6	312	66.4	$$512	$436
51 General and Operations Managers	1,007	29.9	301	66.9	$1,354	$972
TWO THIRDS OF WOMEN WORKERS						

Notes:

* Wages reflect only full-time workers. In 2010, of 65,705,000 women who worked full time or part time, 44,472,000 worked full time.

** The Department of Labor does not report data on populations of less than fifty-thousand people. These jobs have fewer than fifty-thousand workers of the indicated gender.

Source: WOW Analysis of U.S. Department of Labor, Bureau of Labor Statistics, Annual Averages, 2010, http://www.bls.gov/cps.

Why women are concentrated and stuck in low-wage work is a complex and gendered quandary. For decades, researchers have demonstrated that the skills associated with service work (which comprises a significant portion of the low-wage market)—the emphasis on sociability, caring, nurturance, communicating, and making customers feel good, for instance—are frequently deemed to be natural feminine qualities, and the skills required on these jobs are typically unnoticed and poorly rewarded in the labor market. Not surprisingly, the data show that the service jobs that emphasize these skills are often filled by women and characterized by low wages and limited opportunities for advancement. These jobs typically represent the only opportunities for single mothers, especially those who are on welfare or recently off of it. There is a great deal of evidence that education and training, along with access to career ladders and income supports, are key to moving out of the low-wage market.[39] And so, I wanted to find out if the public workforce development system intended to provide venues for these stepping stones, or if it actually keeps women stuck in low-wage work.

It is not just that women have been concentrated in low-wage and low-quality work, it is that these jobs are the ones that are growing in availability. Table I.2 highlights the very gendered nature of the occupations that are projected to have the largest growth in the next few years. First, women represent at least 50 percent of the workforce in eighteen of the twenty-nine occupations with the largest projected job growth, and over 70 percent in thirteen of these occupations. In the top ten occupations with largest projected job growth, women constitute at least 50 percent of the workforce in all but two of the occupations (postsecondary teachers and construction laborers).

Second, women are over-represented in the growing-number occupations that are also among the lowest-paying occupations. Fourteen of the twenty-nine growth occupations have low or very low earnings. Among the top ten projected growth occupations, seven have low or very low earnings. So not only are many of the occupations traditionally female occupations, they are also low wage. Further, many of these occupations do not have benefits, health care, pensions, paid sick days,

TABLE I.2. Occupations with the largest projected job growth, 2008–2018

Occupation	Median Annual Wage Quartile, 2008	Percentage Female, 2010	Percentage Black, 2010	Percentage Hispanic, 2010
Registered Nurses	VH	91.0	12.0	4.9
Nursing, Psychiatric, and Home Health Aides	VL	88.2	34.6	14.7
Customer Service Representatives	L	66.6	17.5	15.2
Combined Food Preparation and Serving Workers, including Fast-food	VL	61.3	12.8	16.6
Personal and Home Care Aides	VL	86.1	23.8	17.6
Retail Salespeople	VL	51.9	11.3	13.7
Office Clerks, General	L	84.2	13.0	15.6
Accountants and Auditors	VH	60.1	8.6	5.8
Post-secondary Teachers	VH	45.9	6.3	5.0
Construction Laborers	L	2.7	9.0	43.1
Preschool and Kindergarten Teachers	H	81.8	9.3	7.3
Driver/Sales Workers and Truck Drivers	H	4.6	13.6	17.5
Grounds Maintenance Workers	L	5.8	6.3	43.8
Bookkeeping, Accounting, and Auditing Clerks	H	90.9	6.5	8.8
Secretaries and Administrative Assistants	H	96.1	8.6	9.4
Management Analysts	VH	43.7	7.2	6.7
Computer Software Engineers	VH	20.9	5.1	3.9
Receptionists and Information Clerks	L	92.7	9.8	16.8
Carpenters	H	1.4	4.0	25.7
Medical Assistants, Other Health Care Support	L	89.7	17.8	16.4
First-line Supervisors or Managers of Office and Administrative Support Workers	H	68.7	9.7	11.1
Network Systems and Data Communications Analysts	VH	26.2	6.6	6.7
Licensed Practical and Vocational Nurses	H	91.7	24.4	6.2
Security Guards and Gaming Surveillance Officers	L	20.8	28.8	15.9
Waiters and Waitresses	VL	71.1	7.1	16.6
Maintenance and Repair Workers, general	H	3.8	11.1	18.0
Physicians and Surgeons	VH	32.3	5.8	6.8
Child Care Workers	VL	94.7	16.0	19.1
Teacher Assistants	L	92.4	12.7	15.1

Note: VH = Very High; H = High; L = Low; VL = Very Low;

Source: U.S. Bureau of Labor Statistics, "Occupational Employment Projections to 2018," 2010, http://www.bls.gov/opub/mlr/2009/11/art5full.pdf.

advancement opportunities, and other supports to help workers attain economic security and family well-being. Perhaps most distressing is that these occupations represent some of the most vulnerable workers, who are performing the work that cares for the most vulnerable in our society and, actually, all of us. And that is the greatest irony—those that care for others often find themselves unable to support themselves and their families. And it is these women that found themselves in the One Stops trying to do just that. They were often unemployed or very underemployed and in the need of services.

These national trends are quite evident in New Jersey, the state in which I conducted my research. Focusing on New Jersey's economy also highlights important structural factors that had an impact on the women I came in contact with during my research. Before the recession began, New Jersey was at nearly full employment, with an unemployment rate of just over 4 percent. In fact, the state's unemployment rate was under 5 percent before 2008. However, the profile of New Jersey's unemployed has changed since the onset of the recession. In 2011, total unemployment was more than two times greater than in 2007, and long-term unemployment was more than five times greater. Not only did New Jersey's unemployment rate rise dramatically during the recession, people also were remaining unemployed longer. Just over half of all unemployed residents in 2011 (215,000) were considered long-term unemployed (those unemployed for more than twenty-six weeks).[40]

When one looks across categories of gender, an important story emerges from the New Jersey economy. The unemployment rate for men peaked in 2010 and, at 9.7 percent, was unchanged in 2011. Similar to national gender trends during the economic recovery, the male share of total unemployment in New Jersey decreased slightly from 57.5 percent in 2007 to 55.1 percent in 2011. The increase in the overall unemployment rate in the state between 2009 and 2011 was primarily due to an increase in women's unemployment.[41]

Women also fared worse than men in regard to the length of their joblessness in New Jersey. In 2007, one-third of the long-term unemployed were women. By 2011, women's share of the long-term unemployed had increased to 45 percent. The data are staggering. In 2007, only 16 percent of unemployed women were long-term unemployed; by 2011 that had drastically increased to 50 percent.[42] Given the national and state data, then, it is not surprising that unemployment, reemployment, and the opportunities available in the labor market have dominated the anxieties that men and women are feeling and that contributed to an even more daunting task faced by front-line workers in the One Stop Career Center.

Theoretical Frame

While the structural challenges of the labor market illustrate the gravity of the situation and guided my research, I went into the field with a critical policy framework of the workforce system. I borrow heavily from a seminal book, *Street Level Bureaucracy*, which provides an approach that reverses the traditional premise of the hierarchy that is often subscribed to government programs.[43] The author, Michael Lipsky, notes that under certain circumstances it is useful to regard the bureaucrats at the bottom of the ladder as actual policymakers. He suggests that lower-level bureaucrats can make policy in many ways. For example, their statuses are ambiguous, and contradictory policies require discretionary decision making at the front-line point of delivery. Further, the routine activities of front-line workers cannot be fully monitored or controlled. When it comes to workforce policy, this has an impact on what level of service a client is referred to or what job leads that person receives, both of which are central to his or her ability to reach economic security.

Lipsky offers an approach to the policy process that I find quite useful. He suggests that the policy process is created from the interactions of individuals inside the agencies who are delivering the policy to clients. He presents an analytical challenge to investigate policy as it is produced in real time and the factors shaping it. This approach has been extended and enhanced by several others. University of Chicago professor Evelyn Brodkin, for instance, notes that this critical policy approach allows one to separate "policy fact from policy fiction." The policy fiction is the policy rhetoric, the ascribed intent of the policy. She provides the example of welfare policy's rhetoric "to prepare clients for work," along with the administrative constructs used as proxies (placements and participation rates). Street-level bureaucracy, she argues, requires that if researchers wish to attribute outcomes to policy they need to be able to specify the policy intervention, not as imagined or reconstructed in administrative measures, but as it is experienced, requiring different evaluation methods.[44] This approach has been further refined by policy scholars who have noted that the production of policy is actually a co-production. This highlights the roles both front-line workers *and* clients play as producers and coproducers in bureaucratic encounters. Given that, a key aspect of my research was to include interviews and focus groups with the front-line workers at the One Stop Career Center to understand the ways in which workforce policies are experienced and implemented daily.

Anthropologist Sandra Morgen has argued how the role of welfare workers as active agents in shaping welfare policy during welfare reform is marked by both devolution and privatization. These processes have downsized the role of the state in regulation of the market. As a result of devolution, which transfers government functions from higher levels to lower levels of the federal hierarchy, not only has the federal government shrunk, but also vacuums materialized in policies at the lower, often local, levels. And privatization, with an increased contracting out of services to profit and nonprofit agencies, only serves to widen these vacuums. These more macro-level policy processes open up an environment in which "how and sometimes even whether, policy is implemented depended on the front line workers who carry out policy in their day to day work."[45]

Similar to Brodkin, Morgen, and others, I enhance this critical policy approach with a feminist lens of understanding the lived experiences of female clients within a broader gendered social structure, to ensure that the voice of the client is part of the policy process and analysis. While there is a growing body of research on welfare reform that focuses on the lives of welfare recipients themselves, the same is not true of workforce development policy. One cannot just take the findings of welfare policy and assume them to be similar to workforce development policy, even if some of the clients may have similar demographic compositions. Political scientist Nancy Fraser among others has pointed out that there is a two-tiered official welfare system—Temporary Assistance for Needy Families (TANF) and Social Security insurance—and argued that this translates into a hierarchy of social citizenship. Clients in the public assistance programs endure administrative humiliations, whereas social insurance clients are seen as paying customers. This latter group qualifies for citizenship in virtually the fullest sense of the term in a male-dominated capitalistic society.[46]

Yet it is unclear where workforce development policy and its clients fall. Unemployment is an insurance system, not a means-tested entitlement. The WIA is premised on universal access—meaning anyone regardless of age, education, income, and occupation can use its services. In fact, one does not even need to be unemployed to access services. Yet at the same time, unemployment is socially stigmatizing in a Protestant ethic work world, and, as sociologist Ofer Sharone suggests, the process of finding new employment continues to stigmatize the job seeker. Sharone argues that American workers, and particularly professional workers, must engage in a "chemistry game"—in which the focus is not as much on hard skills but on demonstrating one's interpersonal fit with a potential employer. In his study of unemployed white-collar workers during the current recession, Sharone finds that such a framework

make[s] American job seekers highly vulnerable to self-blame. This turns unemployment into a double crisis: In addition to the financial crisis of wondering how one will keep paying the bills and not lose one's home, there is the personal crisis of wondering "What's wrong with me?" Moreover, on top of the emotional turmoil, self-blame also generates secondary effects that are no less important, including a profound sense of discouragement about the utility of further job searching.[47]

In addition to the emotional and psychological aspects of unemployment, if you have ever been in a One Stop Career Center, you may have noticed that they sometimes can be drab physical spaces, reminding one much more of a welfare office than a career center. Plus, with the co-location of social services in many states, the welfare and workforce offices are sometimes in the same geographic space. While this may facilitate service delivery and integration, which is a good thing, it blurs the boundaries between programs. This blurring can be problematic if social service and workforce systems are stratified in public opinion and social citizenship. Further, although there is universal access, clients are typically framed as being low income and low skilled (although this appears to be changing in the current recession), and many of the services that are available in One Stop Career Centers are basic job search skills development to ensure that workers are "ready to work," even though they had to have worked in order to qualify for their unemployment insurance.

These contradictions reinforce the fact that, as noted, it is unclear where workforce development policy and its clients fall in the social services system. While it is true that the WIA is premised on universal access and anyone can access some of its basic services, most people find themselves at a One Stop Career Center because they become unemployed; in fact some individuals may be required to participate in workforce activities as a stipulation of their unemployment insurance. The unemployment insurance system, enacted in 1935, has always been thought of as a program for people who demonstrated their attachment to the workforce and were temporarily and involuntarily out of a job. However, in 1935 this system was developed for traditional male workers—white male breadwinners. As an insurance program, and not an assistance program, its benefits are based on an employment relationship and typically are offered only to workers with well-established employment experience via payroll taxes.[48]

Historically, then, many marginalized individuals and workers were never considered to be "deserving" of unemployment insurance benefits. Some of this was tied to racism, as workers in agricultural fields and domestic service were originally excluded from unemployment insurance as a "matter of course," with policymakers claiming that the administrative difficulties of collecting such data were insurmountable. Yet this explanation did not hold much water, given that policymakers at the time refused to entertain feasible models from other countries that provided strategies that include these workers in unemployment insurance programs. By not incorporating such models, it is clear that this decision was more about ensuring that the new unemployment insurance programs did not interfere with the exploitation of African American and female labor in the sharecropping and domestic services.[49] In addition, because unemployment insurance eligibility must be related to the work itself or the employment relationship, women who have to leave the workforce for caregiving reasons cannot access the insurance program, a factor that still applies today. Over the years, states have added additional eligibility requirements tied to earnings requirements, hours worked, and employment patterns. Unemployment insurance has been and continues to be structured to fit male work patterns. "The ideal worker, according to the unemployment insurance system, experiences unemployment only when laid off, not because of being faced with a choice between going to work or staying home to care for a sick child. . . . This ideal employee makes more than a low wage and holds a full time job."[50]

However, at the same time, despite the fact that policymakers have selected out "undeserving" workers from unemployment insurance, unemployment is still socially stigmatizing for those "deserving" workers, even in an economic recession. And in the current recession there were numerous reports of employers weeding out unemployed applicants for perspective jobs, regardless of skills and education. So it is quite nebulous exactly where workforce development falls within a stratified social citizenship of public policy, and this contradictory position of clients casts a shadow on them as they access unemployment and workforce services.

Further, even though 48 percent of workforce development clients are women,[51] their outcomes and experiences are quite affected by gender assumptions and social structures.[52] Over twenty years ago, feminist author Dorothy Smith argued for the importance of taking women's standpoints into account to meet policy goals that are directed toward them. As Smith noted, "our culture does not arise spontaneously; it is manufactured. The ideological apparatuses are part of the larger relations of ruling the society, the relations that put it together, coordinate its work, manage its economic process, generally keep it running, and regulate and control it. Since the positions of power are almost exclusively held by men, men's perspectives, needs, interests, and experiences are represented as general and natural."[53] When women's standpoints are not acknowledged, men—and in particular white men—are the ones who then define women's needs and experiences, and develop the policy and programmatic responses intended to address those needs.

Because women's experiences are marginalized and excluded in public policy discourses, the policies themselves are often constructed in ways that reproduce traditional gender ideology and relations. Indeed, it is not until women's standpoints are integrated into policy formation and analysis that hidden (and sometimes not that hidden) ideologies that underlie policy can begin to be revealed, along with the ways men and women may experience that policy intervention. Sociologist Heidi Gottfried and political scientist Laura Reese urge that gender must be brought into analytical focus in policy work, as "gender enters both into the framing of policy and its differential impacts."[54] They note that distinct from traditional policy work, a feminist policy analysis questions "how gender is constructed in welfare state policies and how these policies are a force in ordering gender relations."[55] Increasingly more sophisticated feminist policy analyses explore how gender and other variables (such as race, class, or marital status) intersect and form axes of oppression, creating unique experiences for different groups of women.[56] In doing so, an intersectional lens establishes that women are not an undifferentiated category.[57] Public policies then not only differentially affect women as compared to men, but also privilege certain groups of women over other women.

The framework guiding my investigation therefore takes into account the problematic nature of workforce development policy, along with the uncertainty of exactly where clients fall within a stratified social citizenship of public policy, and the impact of gendered assumptions of the welfare and workforce development systems. Further, I conducted this research at a particular moment in time with high levels of unemployment across the economy. This framework therefore made this an interesting theoretical and ethnographic project, but it also is quite practical in the search for ways to improve the way policy is delivered. It makes it necessary to understand what is happening at the front lines of workforce policy through the standpoints and lived experiences of clients and front-line workers.

Organization of the Book

To share my journey, I have organized this book in ways to detail the richness of my participant observation yet ensure that the stories are grounded in the critical policy discussion. I begin with the lived experiences of the workers and clients, along with my own observations, in order to demonstrate what was occurring in the field. I then turn to a larger discussion of the broader workforce system, putting it in historical context. Finally, I move to a discussion of where things currently stand and what course should be followed from here. In Chapter 1, "Navigating the System," I share my experiences and the experiences of other clients as we navigate the One Stop Career Center system. This chapter explores the experiences from the moment one walks into the One Stop Career Center after applying for unemployment insurance to the interactions with staff to attending numerous classes and seminars to become "job ready" (despite the fact that most clients have held many jobs) to options for training and education.

In this chapter I focus on the diversity of clients who come to the One Stop Career Center—both low-skilled, low-income clients (who may or may not previously have been welfare recipients) and higher-skilled and educated clients. Both of these groups of workers have particular challenges in the labor market and the workforce development system. Low-skilled workers' experiences are particularly troubling, as the movement away from a policy of skills development orientation to one of workforce delivery systems that has occurred over the past decades has led to countless low-skilled clients remaining stuck in low-wage work, without access to the resources necestsary to secure education and skills training needed to advance into higher-paying jobs. When the recession hit, these workers' already precarious economic situations worsened with job losses or reduced work hours. Grounding this larger research in workforce policy and social services, I draw on my interview and participant observation data of lower-skilled clients to focus on two main themes—clients being "lost in the system" and the dehumanization process clients often endure—in order to detail their experiences and access to workforce services. In this way I tease out the larger implications for clients' long-term prospects for economic security and social citizenship, particularly in an economically vulnerable time of a "Great Recession."

Drawing on my interviews, focus groups, and participant observation data, this chapter then also explores the challenges of higher-educated and skilled workers as they use a system that is often geared toward entry-level employment. Throughout this chapter I focus on key challenges these workers face, including finding workforce services that are applicable to higher-skilled workers, the disconnect between the client's background and the available jobs via the public workforce system, and the emotional frustrations that clients experience. I use the experiences of clients, along with my own participant observation, to explore the tensions between the WIA as a public workforce policy charged with providing universal access to all individuals regardless of education or occupation and actual practices on the ground at the One Stop Career Centers that continue to treat all clients as low skilled. As economic difficulties spread to more and more of the population, individuals who may never have imagined themselves as part of the public workforce system now find themselves sitting in One Stop Career Centers and accessing services. The One Stop Career Centers become intermixing geographic locations of individuals of various educational levels, ages, and socioeconomic classes, yet most clients are often viewed within a narrow lens of "welfare recipient," as opposed to "career center client." And the movement to a workforce development system with a predominant focus on the low skilled is neither helping the low skilled nor addressing the diversity of individuals entering the One Stops.

Chapter 2, "On the Front Line During a Recession," tells the stories of the counselors and caseworkers who are on the front line in the One

Stop system. Using this framework, I explore how front-line workers viewed their jobs of finding people work during the recession. Front-line workers report that they understand the challenges of the economy and social structures, but in practice have internalized a very individualistic approach to the clients—specifically, that the clients need to be realistic about their options, take personal responsibility for their situation, and do whatever it takes to get any job. Such an approach is very much in line with the ideological underpinnings of welfare reform that emphasizes personal responsibility. Further, as workforce services become increasingly compartmentalized, front-line workers rarely are able to address the full needs of clients, nor can they stay with a client as he or she progresses through the workforce system. Instead they address just a piece of the client's employment needs and depend on referrals for the clients to other services. Some have argued that this has created a de-skilling of front-line workers, as they simply match up clients with available jobs, training, or services, regardless of clients' needs or skills.

The chapter concludes with a discussion of the emotional labor workers engage in on a daily basis as they try to find clients jobs in the recession. Front-line staff members report the emotional challenges they face as they see client after client tell their stories of job loss in their offices and their difficulties in locating new work. On-the-job stress and emotional labor are often ignored in the bureaucracy of the workforce system. Yet, during this recession in particular, it is important to take the lived experiences of workers into account and find ways to help workers cope psychologically and emotionally.

Chapter 3, "Understanding the Backstory of Workforce and Welfare Policy," brings together the stories and experiences of unemployed workers and the front-line staff at the One Stop Career Center with a broader discussion of workforce policy and, in particular, its gendered and racialized history. The experiences that I report on did not occur in a vacuum. Government policy both current and past informed and shaped them. Ideas about employability for certain groups in our society, deservedness of social supports, and view of motherhood, among other factors, influence government policy and programs. Remnants of racism and sexism from the past, along with existing structural inequality, have an impact on who gets what services, and why they do. As sociologist Sharon Hays has noted, our national laws represent our national values.[58] So understanding how our nation views unemployed workers, and particularly women, one must understand how it is ingrained in our social policies. In this chapter I trace public employment and training dating back to the New Deal policies, to uncover these values and how they inform the current workforce and welfare legislation. Coupling this with an understanding of the lived experiences of both the clients and workers that I chronicled in my participant observation helps to better discern the impact of racism and sexism, and the existing formulations of public policy.

And in the final chapter, "Charting a Course Forward," I explore what can be learned from the experiences of clients and job counselors in order to improve the delivery of workforce services and help get individuals into good-paying jobs. In doing so I highlight the impact of some changes in the daily practices of the One Stop Career Center I explored, but also the limits of the changes at the local level. I demonstrate how my findings of the daily practices and interactions in the field highlight the need for larger and significant macro-level policy changes for the workforce system to truly meet the needs of clients, front-line workers, and employers.

CHAPTER 1

Navigating the Workforce System

The first time that I walked into the One Stop Career Center under-cover, I had my cover story well rehearsed. My alias was Mary Jones, and I was posing as a woman who had recently relocated to the Jersey Shore. Prior to my move I had worked as a waitress for several years. I came to the One Stop Career Center because I had lost my job when I moved and was looking for waitressing work to support myself and my family. I purposely chose waitressing for two reasons. First, I had worked as a waitress for years in college and graduate school. During that time, I also had conducted research on the food service industry—later publishing a book and several articles that focused on work processes at restaurants. So I was confident that I could address any questions clients or case managers might ask.

However I had a second, more compelling reason to pose as a wait-ress. Although waitressing may be a seasonal job in which I did my research, it is one that is in high demand for labor in the New Jersey market and nationally. Waiter and waitress jobs are among the occupa-tions the U.S. Bureau of Labor Statistics (BLS) projects to see the most growth through 2020.[1] Yet these are by no means jobs that provide eco-nomic security—the BLS reports that the 2010 median annual income is $18,330. Basic economic security includes the ability to afford hous-ing, utilities, food, transportation, child care, health care, emergency and retirement savings, and other personal expenses.[2] Individuals who are not paid enough to meet these basic needs must pick and choose which needs are met daily. Emergency expenses become tremendous strains, and basic expenses, such as food and electricity, can become a burden. In New Jersey, where I was posing as a waitress, I could expect to earn a base wage of $2.13 an hour—the federal subminimum wage for tipped workers. So, as a waitress, the bulk of my income would be earned from tips—which rise and fall with the tides of people that ebb in and out of the shore.

My colleagues at Wider Opportunities for Women (WOW) developed the Basic Economic Security Tables (BEST) wage index to better understand economic insecurity. They found that 45 percent of all Americans live in households that lack economic security, like my alternate self.[3] Eighty-eight percent of adult servers who worked in 2011 had individual earnings below the BEST threshold for their families. Of these individuals, 83 percent are women. Looking across gender, WOW found that 90 percent of female servers who worked in the previous twelve months had individual earnings below the security line. This means that nine out of ten female servers were not paid enough to enjoy basic economic peace of mind. Among males, this figure stands at 74 percent. Accounting for total household income, 73 percent of adult servers lived in households with earnings below the bar for their families. So even with dual income, the bottom line for families in my assumed line of work did not look much better. And what if I were the main breadwinner in my house? Eighty-one percent of households headed by an adult server have total household incomes below the BEST level for their family. And women head 80 percent of these households—51 percent of them single, and 26 percent of those, single mothers.[4] In other words, almost any way you slice it, it was likely that I would be unable to earn enough money to achieve basic economic security as a server. Knowing that the job I was searching for via the workforce system was not going to offer me economic security, I was interested to see how One Stop staff would react to my choice; I wanted to see if the workers there would guide me to skills training, jobs, or both that could better provide for my future.

In this chapter, I first share the experiences of low-wage and low-skilled clients, many of whom were single mothers whom I met during my time as a participant observer in the One Stop system. Like my waitress identity, these clients often need additional training or other education to enter into jobs that can provide economic security. Yet the workforce system cannot always provide those resources, and instead many clients are directed right back into low-wage work—exacerbating an already tenuous economic situation. And many of these same were profiled by the unemployment system as "likely to exhaust unemployment benefits." This means that, on the basis of their education, work experience, age, and other factors, they had a good chance of remaining on unemployment for the full ninety-nine weeks.

However, low-skilled workers are only one group coming to the One Stop Career Centers. To fully understand the experiences of clients, I wanted to get a sense of what it would be like for clients with higher skills and education. In this chapter I also juxtapose my undercover work as a waitress in the One Stop Career Center with complementary undercover work in which I posed as a researcher and teacher holding advanced degrees trying to navigate that same system. I also conducted focus groups with women with either college education or decades of work experiences at managerial levels in order to see how representative my undercover work was. These two composites of women illustrate some of the key clients walking into the One Stop Career Center doors—and I wanted to try to represent their experiences.

What Is Inside the One Stop Career Center?

To prepare for my visit to the One Stop Career Center, it was helpful for me to know the possible services available to workers in New Jersey. Such information can be found online at the Department of Labor website, along with printed brochures and fliers that are at public locations such as libraries and other government offices. Not only did I consider that a scan of those resources would aid in identifying what was accessible, in an age in which information is readily available, I assumed that many of my fellow clients would also have done some Internet searching before their visits.

One of the first things I learned was that the One Stop Career Center houses a resource room where many core services are available. Many of these services are self-directed by the client, while a smaller number of services are staff assisted. Here I should also expect to find banks of computers with Internet access. This enables clients to search for occupational background information, to job search, and to post resumes. In addition, the brochures noted that the computers also have Microsoft Office suites, so that individuals can, for instance, use Microsoft Word for typing letters, resumes, and other employment applications. Further, there are printers available, but the materials I came across did stress that this was only for printing employment-related materials. I also discovered that I could use the computers to set up and check an email account for my job search. Other forms of technology that I would be able to use included a table of telephones, for contacting employers and other employment-related calls; a fax machine, for job applications, resumes, and other employment-related materials; and a copier, for photocopying employment-related materials. Access to computers and online resources were heavily touted as important available and free resources.

In addition, I learned that there was a physical bulletin board on which local area job listings and Civil Service listings were posted (the job listings are updated on Mondays). Finally, in the resource room would be on-site recruitments; here bulletin boards would post advertisements of the schedule of employers coming to the One Stop Career Center to interview job applicants. The other large public space in the One Stop was the Workplace Learning Link—this, I learned, is the staff-assisted workplace literacy program, which also is open to all individuals who come to the One Stop center. In the Workplace Learning Link are banks of computers on which clients can learn at their own pace, in order to gain basic computer skills; learn how to read and communicate better; improve math skills; and learn how to use the Internet.

There was also a series of classrooms in which staff conducted workshops. These workshops include resume writing, self-management, training and labor market, and other information services. Finally, there are also private offices, where the clients would meet one on one with frontline staff to receive individual help with resume-writing techniques, interviewing tips, mock interview exercises, conducting an effective job search, occupational choice counseling, and referral to other agencies.

It was also clear from these materials that there would be additional resources from other departments available to me at the One Stop Career Center. This conglomeration of departments is often referred to as the co-location of services from other departments and organizations in the One Stop Career Centers and includes job corps, veteran's services, the division of vocational rehabilitation, aging services, social services, and unemployment. However, despite having offices, it did not mean that they were staffed fully—as was clear from the brochures and website I looked at before my visit. Instead there might be specific times when staff were available.

Having a good sense of the services available in the One Stop Career Center I would be attending, I was eager to know if the services and organizations I would experience would be typical of those in other states. Interestingly, while there have been some very strong case studies of particular One Stops in certain states,[5] there appears to be no comprehensive source that details the ways that different state and local One Stops are organized. Further, University of Chicago professor Carolyn Heinrich and her colleagues point out that "the latitude in WIA [Workforce Investment Act] that states have used to structure the One Stop system reflects the local preferences under the direction of the local agency, the WIB [Workforce Investment Board], stressing that there are wide variations across localities."[6] To give one example, economists Burt Barnow and Christopher King in their case study of eight workforce systems note that how the relationship between the WIA and Temporary Assistance for Needy Families (TANF), which is listed as an optional One Stop partner in the WIA legislation, is actually organized in the local state system depends on state and local goals, program philosophy, management style, and political culture.[7] For instance, in Florida, Michigan, Texas, and Missouri, the state workforce development agency receives and spends the state's TANF workforce development funds, while in Utah the state workforce agency controls all TANF funds. TANF is a mandatory partner in Oregon and Missouri, but the relationship is not as strong as in other states. In Indiana and Maryland, TANF is an optional partner, and TANF's presence in the centers varies across local areas.[8]

These differences in organization of workforce services make nation-wide studies more difficult, and have led many to point out "there is no simple picture of what services a customer receives under WIA."[9] Instead, much of the research has been case studies on one or several states. However, while there is not one model of One Stop Career Centers, there are similarities in the services that are offered and the ways they may be organized. So case studies can highlight organizations and practices that are effective in places. My ethnographic work is framed in a similar vein—trying to understand what is happening at the ground level in the One Stop I am in, while also being able to extrapolate and highlight larger structural factors.

My First Day as an Unemployed Waitress

Ready to begin my undercover research, I headed into the One Stop Career Center on a cold spring day. On the basis of the descriptions in the brochures and websites I had studied, my mental picture was that the One Stop would be more of a career center, perhaps similar to what one may have access to at a college. However, one of the first things I noticed was that a One Stop Career Center can be a drab physical space—reminiscent of a welfare office and *not* a career center. As soon as I walked in the door I saw a large sign telling me to check in at a receptionist's desk. I was actually taken aback to see that right next to this desk stood a security officer.[10] Yet while it was a bit disconcerting to be greeted this way, I came to learn that other One Stops throughout the country welcome clients by requiring them to walk through a metal detector. The reasoning is to protect both clients and workers, but it certainly sets a tone of insecurity and fear.

I stood in line, and when I got to the receptionist's desk, I told her that I was there to attend the reemployment seminar. I was excited about this seminar, because it is usually the first class a client attends to learn about the One Stop services and resources. The receptionist, barely looking up at me, gave me the room number, and I headed into a room that reminded me of a high school classroom. There was an instructor's desk in the front, with rows of tables and chairs facing it. The seminar was scheduled to begin at 2:00 P.M., but when I entered the room at 1:55 P.M., there was no instructor in the room. After I found a seat, I noticed that there were three stacks of papers on the table in the front of the room. A female client, who was sitting in the front, said that I needed to take the papers and sign in on the sign-in sheet. I did that. In fact, as others walked into the room, this female client continued to take the lead in directing them to sign in and to take the sheets. After some time passed she even joked, "Maybe they should give me a job!"

The three forms were an information sheet that I assumed I was to fill out (although there were no official directions on it), a sheet on the One Stop services with a screen shot of the state Department of Labor website, and a form about the Equal Employment Opportunity Commission regulations. I began to complete the personal information sheet. By then 2:00 P.M. had come and gone and still there was no instructor. At that time there were eighteen of us in the room, all sitting classroom style and looking uncomfortable, nervous, and confused. Finally at around 2:05 the instructor came into the room and announced that she could not get started until 2:10. She then added, "They make us wait." I asked "Why are we getting started at 2:10, when we were told to be here at 2?" She answered, "The unemployment office makes us wait until 2:10 because there will be latecomers. Unemployed people are always late." She added, "If it was up to me, we would start on time." She promised us that the class would be very fast and we would be out quickly. She again stressed that the unemployment office makes the decisions on the start times and that she did not work for them. Then she left the room.

I was shocked by the instructor's response and quickly scanned the expressions of the individuals next to me, noting that they seemed quite embarrassed by the comment. Although the instructor had tried to distance herself from the decision-making process, she had had no qualms about reporting to us that the class was going to start late because of a stereotypical view of unemployed people. And ironically, not one of my classmates for that seminar was late—we all arrived before the 2:00 P.M. start. Once the class *did* begin, it lasted only nine minutes. My classmates and I were stunned. Imagine being able to sum up the vast state and local workforce resources in just nine minutes. It is an impossible task—and in the class we basically learned to check out the website (something I had already done before class). The instructor then prided herself in getting us out of class so quickly. What she did not understand was that the clients in the room were not there just for an unemployment requirement. They wanted information and resources. They were hungry for solid job and labor market leads, and unsure what the next steps should be to become reemployed. Further, many clients had had to arrange transportation and child care—often challenging and costly—to attend the seminar. As we left the classroom that afternoon, we felt just as lost as when we came in. While other orientations that I attended later in my undercover work provided more information, this first stop on my journey presented themes that would continue throughout my research. As I would come to find, this reliance on stereotypes and dehumanization was not unique to this instructor or class.

And, of course, the stereotype of unemployed individuals as lazy and individually flawed was not unique to the One Stop experience. In the job market this stereotype was drastically illustrated by some companies that, during the recession, were biased against the long-term unemployed. Economists Rand Ghayad and William Dickens's research illustrating the Beveridge Curve in the current recession and recovery helped to confirm this. Quite simply, the Beveridge Curve finds that as the number of job openings grows, the number of unemployed should go down. In the current recovery, this was not happening. When Ghayad and Dickens decomposed the curve by length of unemployment they found that the curve shifted up—meaning that more job openings did not translate into lower unemployment for those who were out of work for more than six months. That finding held true across age, industry, and educational level.[11] Further, Ghayad found the same result when he sent out 4,800 fictitious resumes to six hundred job openings, with 3,600 of them for unemployed people. He further varied how long they had been unemployed, how often they switched jobs, and whether they had industry experience. He found that how long a prospective employee was out of work trumped the other factors.

Specifically, if a person was out of work for less than six months, that person would get a call back even if he or she did not have experience; yet if the person were out of work for more than six months, his or her experience did not matter.[12] This stigmatization of the unemployed is something that my fellow clients in that class had to deal with.

Of course, this is not new. It is quite consistent with what women coming off of welfare experience in the labor market. In fact, the connections to welfare policy were not far from my mind when I sat in that class at the One Stop Career Center. First, as I scanned the room and talked informally with clients, it seemed to me that the impact of President Clinton's welfare reform seemed to compound the experiences of many of the women in the room. The work-first policies implemented during 1996 welfare reform primarily used "job placement" as the performance measure of success. Since the goal was to place clients in paid employment, any job was often considered a "good" job, regardless of wages earned, benefits provided, opportunities for advancement, or control over one's hours. As a result many welfare recipients, among then a disproportionate number of single mothers, flooded into the labor market during the late 1990s. In particular, the number of single mothers entering paid work rose by 25 percent between 1993 and 1999. Within this group there was a 50 percent increase in the employment of never-married single mothers.[13]

Similar to my waitress persona, despite the fact that these women were working, they typically did not earn enough money to support themselves and their families. Often they may have had to cobble together more than one job; make difficult decisions to go without food, medicine, or housing at times; accrue insurmountable debt; and risk their health in order to just survive day to day. While the promise of welfare reform to place recipients into jobs had materialized, there was no companion promise of economic self-sufficiency and security. Instead, the reality was that many women just traded in welfare for low-wage jobs, and remain trapped in poverty for years.

When the recession hit, these workers' already precarious economic situations worsened with job losses or reduced work hours, with some going back on public support. Many of the clients then found themselves on the workforce development side. However, in a work-first world it seems the workforce side has some of the same characteristics as the welfare side. Despite the fact that I knew I should be able to access services, and that I had paid into an unemployment insurance system, I actually felt quite stigmatized as I used these universal services. While I may have been entering the public system as a workforce client, I very much felt like a welfare client. And as other women on welfare have experienced, when I spoke to the instructor and other front-line workers throughout my participation observation about my reemployment plan based on my waitressing background, I found that they expected that I should be able to find restaurant work in the area. In fact, one staff member was excited to tell me about a seasonal job fair that was occurring on the boardwalk near the beachfront—confident that I should be able to locate work there.

While the seasonal job fair or a local waitressing job could have met my immediate need for employment, chances are that it would not have led to economic security or even steady employment. My work skills were in high demand, they just were not considered skills that were high or even moderate wage. This contradiction is a significant factor of the nation's workforce system. If a client has skills to qualify for certain jobs, and there are employment opportunities available among those jobs, the client can be served by the WIA's core services and often will not get to career counseling or training. The staff members who suggested the summer job fair or local restaurant work were doing their jobs. And if I were a client with restaurant background and experience, and was placed in a waitressing job, I would be considered a successful placement, especially in a difficult labor market. Yet although I would then have a job, I would not have economic security or even be out of the realms of the working poor. Recall that the BLS median income of restaurant servers is at $18,330—not enough to be self-sufficient. And once I was employed, my access to some other supports—such as unemployment insurance, child care assistance, or food stamps—could be reduced or eliminated, which would actually exacerbate my economic insecurity.

Further, the insecurity of low-wage restaurant work would provide me with few long-term pathways to economic security. Chances were high that my job would be seasonal (perhaps three to four months during the summer months), and that I would find myself back at the One Stop Career Center just a few months later, as the summer tourist season turned into the fall and winter. Perhaps I would be directed to the Holiday Job Fair at the local mall to explore seasonal retail jobs for the Christmas holidays. My customer service skills from waitressing would easily translate to selling dresses at a Macy's department store or greeting cards at Hallmark. But then as the retail season slowed down, usually after Valentine's Day, I could easily be back in the same unemployed position waiting for the seasonal restaurant jobs to begin hiring for the summer.

One can see how someone like my waitress persona—Mary Jones—can end up in a cycle of churning through low-wage service jobs. During that time she will consistently lack economic security and she typically will not have access to health care, paid sick days, retirement savings, and career advancement. But she will be employed—and if that is the important measure of success, then she will be considered a successful placement. And perhaps she might get lucky that one of the seasonal jobs will turn into full-year work. At least for a short period.

Are You Ready to Work?

In a society and workforce system that views success as the personal responsibility of the individual, it is not surprising that policy is grounded in an idea that clients must be "job ready." When low-wage workers become clients of the One Stop system, one of the first assumptions that they must confront is the relatively explicit message that they are not prepared to work and that they need training to be "job ready." Many workers who found themselves unemployed also found themselves in a seminar that was framed as an orientation directed toward the "hard to employ." On the basis of characteristics of their unemployment applications, the state unemployment office assigned them to a special orientation because of concerns that they would have extreme difficulty finding a job and that they would be likely to exhaust their unemployment benefits. But I only found this out after conversations with work-force officials. When I attended that orientation, the content of the orientation was the same as the other basic orientations, apart from our being told by the instructor that we were assigned to this group because "Unemployment thought [we] would have an extra hard time finding a job." This fact was not lost on my fellow unemployed workers, some of whom were assigned to a general orientation and also the "hard to employ" orientation; these women noted themselves that they could not tell the difference between the courses, nor understand why they were hearing the same information twice.

The WIA, like welfare reform policy with its work-first approach, assumes that the individual shares the bulk of the responsibility for why she or he is not employed, and does not attend to other factors that affect one's ability to secure a job and be economically self-sufficient. Therefore, the interventions for WIA recipients focus on how they must change to find *any* job, and not how education and training can provide human capital to improve their lives. To accomplish this, the core service of the WIA then provides potential workers with what are referred to as "job readiness skills." These "exercises reflected the belief that women on welfare lacked the 'soft skills' or job-related social skills required to find job leads and to overcome the hurdle of a job interview. A lack of hard skills, work-related technical knowledge, and expertise that would require education was not considered problematic."[14] Sharone in his ethnographic research at a California One Stop Center labeled this "the diligence game." Examining the experiences of blue-collar workers in workshops, he found that the focus for job seekers was not so much on objective skills and education, but on whether individuals were eager, compliant, and committed hard workers. And the soft skills were repeatedly coded as an "attitude"—whether the job seeker is motivated to work hard and will do whatever is asked of him or her in a manner that is cheerful, obedient and diligent.[15] That is what it means to be "job ready."

Of course, such thinking obscures the lives of women, and in particular single mothers, which has an impact on job prospects. Most notably, child care demands—finding affordable, adequate, and accessible child care—limit single mothers' job opportunities. In addition, transportation can also be a significant barrier. Nationally, one-third of households earning less than $15,000 a year do not own a car.[16] This is especially relevant in suburban and rural areas with limited public transportation systems, as the very act of getting to a job can be a challenge. And this discussion of structural factors such as child care and transportation seems too often trumped by the idea that a lack of being job ready is the real reason one is unemployed.

Despite these real structural challenges there was a clear understanding that the key to the labor market success was "self-management." In one of the workshops I attended, the materials we were provided helped us work through "self-defeating" thoughts. They provided us with a list of these thoughts—such as "I am too old to get a job" or "I hate change." They then encouraged us to think of ways to change these thoughts and turn them into positive self-talk. Social critic Barbara Ehrenreich[17] offers a broad critique of the positive thinking industry that has emerged in the motivational services offered to unemployed individuals, which pushes the idea that if one experiences joblessness as an opportunity, a positive attitude will help to increase the probability of finding a new job. Of course, the flip side to the positive thinking mantra is that if someone does not have a positive attitude about his or her unemployment, then it is that missing positive attitude that is a contributing factor to their inability to find employment. Such rhetoric easily blames the unemployed for their continued labor market challenges and takes off any pressure to even define unemployment as a jobs issue with a sociological frame. The reality is that even the most positive self-image will not make up for the structural factors of the labor market.

Some of the women I met noted that it was more than just a positive self-image that was recommended to them. For instance, one woman spoke of the emphasis an instructor placed on "dressing." She stated,

She spent so much time in the class talking about what to wear and how bad it looks when people don't dress for interviews. The whole time I was thinking, just get me an interview. I will dress right.

Another woman echoed her point:

Do you know how hard it is to hear someone tell you that you have to be sure to speak a certain way and smile when you talk to your employer? I worked for seventeen years. I didn't get laid off because I can't speak. I got laid off because the store I was working at closed.

In addition, a "job readiness" and positive attitude focus also denies that the low-wage labor market is a significant factor in women's, and in particular, single mothers,' ability to secure work that helps them attain economic self-sufficiency. Indeed, single mothers face a clear structural constraint to their economic viability—that they must earn an income to support themselves and their children *and* provide the unpaid labor to care for their children, often with little or no support. But the jobs in which women are located are overwhelmingly in the low-wage labor market. Remember from Table I.1 that in 2010 the occupations in which most American women were located were secretaries and administrative assistants. These women earned a median weekly income of $657. Other occupations in which women are heavily concentrated offer similar low wages. Nursing, psychiatric, and home health aides, occupations that are 88 percent female, have a median weekly wage of $427; child care workers, who are 95 percent female, earn a weekly median income of $398; and the 89 percent of maids and housekeeping cleaners earn a median weekly wage of $376.[18] So having employment in these occupations does not equate to economic security. But these structural and institutional factors seemed less of a concern. Workforce development policy that simply ensures for all clients the core services of resume writing and Internet job search engines, along with classes on social skills, denies not only the complex life situations of low-wage women but also the labor market into which they are forced.[19]

Access to Education and Skills Training

In a work-first world of workforce development policy, in which the bulk of resources are focused on core services, access to education and training can be quite difficult to attain. Within the workforce system, actually, funding is tied to performance measures that make directing resources to any low-wage workers seem unproductive. Some of these measures—such as newly entered employment levels and earnings gains—actually provide disincentives to serving individuals who are already working and instead favor the unemployed or other groups.[20] As a result, fewer individuals have received skills training through the One Stop system under the WIA than under its predecessor the Job Training Partnership Act (JTPA). According to the U.S. Department of Labor, in program year 2000, approximately 50,000 adults received training under the WIA, as compared to 150,000 annually in the final years of the JTPA.[21] These trends continued through subsequent WIA program years. Center for Law and Social Policy researchers Abby Frank and Elisa Minoff noted that single parents, in particular, have experienced a decline of training services under the WIA. For example, in 1998 (the last program year of the JTPA), 43.7 percent of adult training exiters were single parents. By 2000 (the first full year of WIA data), that percentage had fallen to 34.5, and has continued to decline each year since then.[22]

The decline in the numbers of individuals who receive training is directly related to the three-tiered levels of service. Indeed, the WIA appears to be much more of an employment policy (particularly for private sector jobs) than a training policy, as individuals must pass through core and intensive services before they can access new training on occupation-specific skills. As noted earlier, most distressing is that if the client can be employed without training, that client is typically denied access to training. For my waitress alternate self, the employability plan was more waitressing work—education and career advancement were secondary. The WIA's tiered services have the effect of serving as a barrier to skills training for many single, working-poor mothers who were able to secure entry-level low-wage work. For instance:

A Vermont woman sought the help of the One Stop Career Center after a long history of employment as a housekeeper. Recently divorced and unable to support her family on her housekeeper wages, she wanted to participate in a skilled trades training program to improve her earnings potential. She was turned away because she had had success in the housekeeping field and therefore was not eligible to participate in the training program, which, she was told, was for people with no skills and with a long history of unemployment.[23]

So was what I experienced as an unemployed waitress, and this example from a Vermont housekeeper, happening to other women? The tension between getting a job and getting a job that leads to economic security was evident in many forms. Indeed, several of the women reported to me that they were discouraged from thinking about new careers and instead encouraged to find jobs in the fields that they were in—regardless of the pay. As one woman noted,

Well, I was told we couldn't change careers. We had to only build on what we already knew. I have been in customer service and administration my whole life, so at this point I wasn't able to, say, be a nurse. They said I can only go for updating my skills, not a career change.

Another woman noted she had no choice:

I was ordered to say, you're updating your skills. You are not changing careers.

Yet another woman noted that she was explicitly told that she could not get the training to enter into a new field. During a focus group I asked her, "Did somebody actually say to you that you cannot change your career?" And she responded, "Yes. I cannot get training for a different career." Her experiences were not much different from mine when I attended one of the training seminars at the One Stop Career Center. At this seminar I expected to learn about training options that could be available to me. However, the instructor started off the class by telling us we were in the training class, but stressed, "We are in the business of getting you a job." He further explained that if we possessed skills in demand, we might not be eligible for training. When I asked specifically about my waitressing background, he assured me that I was in a good county to find a waitressing job, with the experience I had. Training is seen as something secondary to placement success.

This is particularly troubling for a variety of reasons. As noted, many of the traditional jobs that women held prior to unemployment did not offer them economic security, and simply returning them to this low-wage work actually compounds their economic situation after months of unemployment. Research clearly shows that training that prepares women for nontraditional jobs also moves them toward economic security, empowerment, and self-development. Such jobs may give them an opportunity to take active control of their lives, and to provide for themselves and their children in a safe and supported way. Careers in nontraditional fields can also provide women with additional knowledge, skills, and resources to become self-sufficient. For example, women in construction and green trades are able to take care of basic home repair; women in mechanical trades can troubleshoot faulty appliances; and women in trades often have higher incomes and better benefits than women in other occupations.

However, many women are being subtly and not so subtly discouraged from considering careers that do offer economic security, particularly jobs that are out of the realm of traditionally female work. For example, one woman who spent years in administrative office support work found herself laid off and wanted to enter into a nontraditional job for women: truck driving. Despite this woman's desire to enter into truck driving, she was steered away from the training that would qualify her for such work. As she told me,

The one thing that I had chosen was definitely a male-dominated field, but there was such a waiting list for that, that they wouldn't even consider it, letting me go to school for that. I was like, I really don't want to do office. I have been doing office since I was twenty-one, nineteen actually.

Her experiences demonstrated the difference between job placement and a pathway to economic security that underlies workforce policy. This distinction was not lost on the clients, as this woman noted:

I was going to go get my CDL [commercial driver's license] because my goal—I know their goal is to get me a job. I know my goal is to make more money, as much money as I can make with my level of education. So, you know, with the CDL, you can make a decent amount of money with that because I am the supporter of my house.

The women knew that the traditional fields that many of them *were* training to take up might not be able to provide them with economic security. One woman training for a certificate to be a medical assistant voiced her thoughts:

I am greatly concerned about the starting rate that I may be offered in this new field. I am concerned about maintaining ownership of my home and running my household with a low starting salary.

As she reported these worries in the focus group, several other women echoed her anxieties. They were also part of the certificate program and were aware of the starting salaries. However they only became aware of them after they were well into their training. While they were grateful for the opportunity to gain a certificate, they were fearful of what their prospects were.

Many of the women I met were not able to access any training or education at all. Within the sequential series of services, eligibility in training programs can be subjective, with education and job training often seen as the last resort, not a core need of all workers. In addition, there is a prescribed menu of options that may or may not fit with the individual's preferences. This point is something that came up often. WIA employment and training services are often tied to high-demand jobs. In New Jersey, such jobs have projected high-growth short-term (less than two years) and long-term (ten years) job openings. Of course this raises the question, What if a client has an interest in a non-demand job? And simply because something is not in high demand, does that mean there is no demand for that job at all? Of course, access to jobs is critical to the workforce system and workers. And if one is to receive training and education, he or she then needs to be employed after completing that training. However, the choices that are then available are limited by demand, and, in particular, high demand. When training is targeted only to high-demand jobs, the client's level of autonomy and choice is affected. For instance, if I wanted to be trained to become a desktop publisher or graphic artist, I would not be able to do that via the workforce system as it was not a targeted high-demand occupation in my local labor market.

The targeted-occupations lists for education and training have been criticized by several policy analysts. Some note that such a policy creates a situation that separates education opportunities into two categories—those that are provided via WIA versus those that are not funded via the workforce system. Underlying this is the understanding that "the free choice that is the hallmark of a market-driven education model is not present under WIA."[24] Instead it is the state that determines which types of education are available to clients in the One Stop system and which educational opportunities are not available to them. While Shaw and Rab note that "there is nothing inherently wrong with developing education and training programs designed to address the needs of the labor market,"[25] when the only education available to WIA clients is what suits the immediate labor needs of employers, then "student choice will be severely constricted despite the free-market philosophy that would, in theory, provide the customer with more choices, rather than fewer."[26]

To have real choices, clients need solid information. Many of the clients were clear on the need for labor market information, education, and skills training, but needed guidance on how to receive it. As one woman told me,

We are not looking for free rides, we understand that one has to earn her education and you can pay back a loan in your future. But it is just the lack of information. Where do you go? Who do you talk to? What is out there? It is just that you want to go to helpme.com and put in what your problem is.

Many of the women reiterated the lack of information they received.

I got nothing. I found out from a friend of mine that said they were going back to school. I don't know how much time I wasted when I could have gone to school. I had no idea. I called them to ask, and they said sometimes we send out letters at random. So, you never know when you are going to get one or not. I said, are you kidding? I was sitting there doing nothing when I could have been in school earlier. I could have been doing other things, but I had no idea that the services were even available.

Indeed, without a clear structure to navigate the system and access resources and information, clients assumed that other factors led to services. For instance, several of the clients noted that "luck" plays a big role in whether one has access to services.

I walked into the One Stop sort of by chance. I was so lucky because they processed me to apply for training. I happened to hit them when they had a little bit of funding. I was lucky, I thought. I found the one to two classes they gave me right away.

The theme of "luck" was also reinforced by staff at the employment center. Several of the women in the focus groups noted that instructors began sessions by stating, "You won the lottery." This meant that they were randomly selected for services. The instructors would go on to suggest to the clients that they might want to play the real lottery, joking that the odds of getting to intensive services were equal to those of buying a winning lottery ticket.

The challenge of trying to integrate client choices into their career future is compounded by institutional bureaucratic factors throughout the U.S. system. This was echoed by members of community organizations around the country who are charged with connecting women to training via the WIA. As one Women Work! community college workforce practitioner testified before Congress,

The One Stop makes our participants jump through too many hoops. It is almost as if they don't want to provide funding for participants to attend school. They seem to make it very difficult for participants to receive services.[27]

The mandate to meet performance measures has a direct impact on the services that clients receive. "Caseworkers pick clients for services on the basis of their perceived ability to complete those services, and find work, rather than on their need for increased skill and education."[28] Quite clearly, such performance-driven practices question individuals' opportunities for education, and instead focus on targeted occupations that are needed for the state's economic benefit, often without consideration of the client's educational and career goals. The focus on short-term job training quite simply has the impact of discouraging long-term educational investments. For example, a study of Illinois welfare recipients found that low-income women would often be discouraged by caseworkers in non-occupation-based training.[29] Even when the WIA does provide access to community college courses, the training is typically short-term, non-degree-bearing, and highly specific job training, despite the clear evidence that there are higher, long-term economic returns for degree and credential granting programs.

There is also the question raised earlier, of the quality of the occupations individuals are being trained to take up. According to the U.S. Department of Labor (USDOL), in 2010 the top ten occupations that WIA clients were trained for were "bright outlook occupations." This meant that these occupations were projected to have greater employment through 2018 than the average occupations. These top ten occupations include (in descending order of workers trained in each) nursing aides, truck drivers, licensed practical nurses, registered nurses, medical assistants, medical records and health information, customer service representatives, health care support occupations, production workers, and computer support workers.[30] While these occupations may be growing in availability, only registered nurses and truck drivers seem to receive economically secure wages. Of course, this is as much an issue of the quality of jobs that are growing as it is a comment on the workforce development system. In fact, this is one of the larger structural issues that came up over and over in my conversations with clients and workers, and to which I will return in later chapters. Quite frankly, the jobs that are available and growing in number tend to be lower wage. At the same time, supports that could make up for lower incomes continue to dwindle. And this leaves both clients and staff in a difficult predicament. So in a time of such economic insecurity, encouraging and training low-wage workers to take up new low-wage jobs needs to be understood and challenged.

While it may be known what occupations individuals are being trained for, it is hard to know exactly who is being served by the WIA because many WIBs do not collect data on the individuals they support. First, what is known? The USDOL reports that nationally there has been an increase in the number of women completing WIA programs from 2008 to 2010. In 2008, 478,429 women exited WIA programs;

by 2010 that number rose to 579,459 women. Among women who were classified as dislocated workers in the WIA system, again there was an increase in exiters—from 174,601 in 2008 to 328,054 in 2010.[31]

While the numbers of women served are known broadly, it is not known how specific categories of women are served. Findings from Wider Opportunities for Women indicate that 35 percent of WIBs do not analyze demographic data, including race, sex, ethnicity, and age of program participants. In addition, 58 percent of WIBs said they did not know if women were placed in nontraditional occupations (occupations that are less than 25 percent female) or whether their agency even had those data available to analyze.[32]

While the WOW/National Association of Workforce Investment Boards study is somewhat dated, its findings are quite instructive. One of the main findings was that overall there is little attention paid to gender in implementing policies. Seventy-three percent of WIBs did not collect data on how displaced homemakers are served disaggregated from information on dislocated workers. About half of the WIBs surveyed did not have representation from organizations that primarily focus on low-income women, making it hard to ensure that women's programs are developed with a gendered lens. This is clearly evident in the disparity between the numbers of displaced homemakers in the United States and the number of those displaced homemakers served by the WIA. Specifically, while census data estimate that over 7.3 million women are displaced homemakers (via divorce, separation, or widowhood), two-thirds of workforce boards report serving fewer than 25 percent of women who fit this category annually. In 2003, at the time of the survey, only 1.5 percent of the dislocated workers population who were provided intensive or training services were displaced homemakers.[33] Women Work! further noted that over 60 percent of women's service providers reported that One Stop service delivery to women in economic transition was poor to fair, as typically One Stop staff lack the expertise and training to effectively serve women with multiple employment barriers. These inequities in services also contribute to the earnings disparity for women exiting the WIA relative to comparable men, with women earning about $1,000 less per quarter.[34] Of course, while this is inextricably tied to the gender wage gap and occupation sex segregation, a lack of attention to gender issues in policy development and implementation, and in particular, a lack of direct focus on nontraditional opportunities for women are significant contributors.

When one looks at different racial categories of women, even more disturbing patterns emerge. Black women on welfare receive far less support with job search education and training than white counterparts, and when they are referred to possible jobs via the public sector, employers treat low-income women differentially on the basis of race.[35] Specifically, black women received shorter interviews; more pre-employment drug tests, criminal background checks, and other checks; greater differences between the job offered and the tasks actually performed; and more evening hour work, and were more likely to report a negative relationship with supervisors.[36] The fact that there is differential access to support services along race and ethnicity is further supported by the National Urban League Institute for Opportunity and Equality. They found that more than 70 percent of Hispanic and African American women did not receive any subsidies (including child care, transportation assistance, and college degree assistance) for work-related activities. In contrast, 62 percent of white women did not receive any subsidies.[37] In addition, sanctions within the public workforce and welfare system are disproportionately leveled against women of color. The Women of Color Policy Network's report found that states with the greatest share of black women on welfare were more likely to impose full family sanctions. As a result, if a mother does something to lose her benefits, her children also lose their benefits. They further reported that while white women were more likely to exit welfare rolls for employment, African American, Latina, and Native American women were more likely to have been sanctioned off the rolls.[38] Findings such as these seriously question how the educational and career needs of single, working-poor mothers, and in particular single, working-poor mothers of color, are met by the current federal employment and training legislation.

Professionals Abound

One of the consequences of framing the workforce system as an extension of the welfare system is that it becomes difficult to fit higher-educated and higher-skilled workers into that framework. As noted earlier, the workforce system is legislatively mandated to be universal, offering a basic level of services for anyone who needs them. Those basic services include job search assistance; labor market information; limited assessments of needs and skills; community asset information; career information; and, in some cases, more in-depth assessments, resume preparation, job clubs, and workshops. During the recession, many workers who had higher skill and education levels, along with sometimes decades of work experience, found themselves at the One Stop Career Centers' doors. To be fair, workers with a college degree did fare better in the labor market than their counterparts who did not have college educations. From 2007 to 2012, unemployment rates for those with just a high school diploma averaged 9.4 percent, while the comparable rate for individuals with a bachelor's degree was less than half—4.5 percent. Unemployment rates for four-year college graduates went up during the recession but never exceeded 6.3 percent, compared to the peak 13.4 percent in February 2010 and the current 9.4 percent unemployment rate for high school graduates.[39] And workers with a high school degree or less bore the brunt of the job losses during the recession, specifically of the 7.1 million jobs lost from 2007 to 2010; over 5.6 million of them were held by someone with a high school degree or less. However, despite those differences there were many workers with college degrees who came to the One Stop Career Center. Yet at times it seemed as if the One Stop staff could not fit these workers into their existing paradigms.

As you may recall from the Introduction, one of the women I spoke with told me that front-line staff members would tell her that because she had a college degree, she therefore was marketable and should be able to go out and get a job. Her experience was not unique. Many of the women I spoke with corroborated her experiences. For instance,

I have been director of operations at [a large company] for over ten years, and when I would go in to the One Stop, they were just like, "Well, keep looking." And it is like, do you understand what I am telling you? I know you sit in this office here, but you must be seeing all of the people coming in and out that don't have jobs who have degrees, have management experience, or professional or intelligent people. It is not just that we are not looking, that we are not utilizing every opportunity.

When the workforce system was forced to address the needs of clients who do not fit a "low-wage worker" mold, workers were often uncertain of the best ways to counsel clients. Suggesting some of the job-ready workshops seemed even more out of place than they did for the lower-skilled clients. This was evident to me when I went to the One Stop with a profile similar to my existing job. I posed as a professor at a local community college who was recently laid off. After the reemployment seminar I attended, I went to talk to the instructor. I told her my employment profile and asked her what my strategy should be. She did not have an answer, and instead said for me to be sure that I was following the correct protocols to ensure my unemployment check would be coming to me. I was prepared for her not to have a response, so then I said, "Well, I am a skilled researcher, so I was thinking of perhaps opening my own business doing research." I then asked her about small business information. Before providing me with anything substantive on the resources available to start a small business, she asked me if I had received my first unemployment check. I told her that I had not. She then said when I did receive it, I should go to room 205 at the One Stop Career Center and they could help me. However they would not be able to help me unless I also showed them several weeks of documented job search. Who exactly made up the "they" was not shared with me at that time. And before I could ask more, she then went on to talk to another client.

As a researcher I wanted to probe this more, but had limited time in that interaction—there was a line of my fellow clients wanting to talk with the instructor, and I had to respect their needs. However, during my focus groups with front-line workers, when I did have the luxury of time, I posed the question to them: "What would you tell me if I came into the One Stop Career Center looking for work? As background I have a Ph.D. in sociology, and my job title is Senior Scholar at a nonprofit policy and research organization in Washington, D.C." The first response I received from one of the workers was "Write a book!" Of course, that made me laugh, as I told them I was currently writing a book, and I had written several others before. Then they said they would suggest I not go the One Stop Career Center for services. As a worker told me,

I refer a lot of people to employment agencies and head hunters. A lot of employers who hire college-educated workers are not really willing to reach out to us at the One Stop. They see us as a regulatory agency for unemployment, disability, and occupational health and safety standards; child labor laws; and immigration, so we are not the first people they think of. I think a private employment agency geared to college-educated workers might have more opportunities.

The workers in the focus group agreed with her. They also went on to say that they would suggest that I build my network as best I can. One worker reported that they suggest to college-educated workers,

You should go back to the college where you received your degrees and education in order to go through their Career Services departments.

In addition to not having the jobs available to suggest to some higher-educated workers, there were other challenges. While workers may have degrees and years of experience, their skills appeared not to match the current labor market demands. One woman noted that she did have a college degree that she received in 1995, in journalism, but, as she states,

I find out that the skills that I earned back in '95 are no longer conducive to what I need to get out there and get a job. So I am started on the same plane that most children are when they get out of high school.

What was frustrating for some of the women who did have college degrees was that it was difficult for them to go back to school as part of the One Stop system. New Jersey does have a tuition waiver program for unemployed workers who need to complete their degrees in a high-demand field. However, if one already has a degree, and is interested in getting a degree in a high-demand field, that person's case would have to go the state Department of Labor in order to receive approval for a waiver. That not only adds time to the process, but, more important, it is far from a guarantee that the request will be granted. This experience was relayed to me by a woman who had a college degree but was only finding low-wage work opportunities. She wanted to go to school to earn a new degree in a field with higher job prospects, but was not able to through the workforce system.

So when I get unemployment and I am begging my counselor to help me go to school—"Hey look, I can't really make it with $15 an hour, is there some type of training I can get or can I see?" I wanted to be a nurse or a teacher. And it took them basically another six months almost to decide whether I could go to school, and I could not.

In the focus group, while hearing this story, the coordinator of the local WIB, sensing the incredible frustration of this client, shared a personal story from her own life. She had been in the room as an unobtrusive observer to learn about what was occurring in the One Stop to help improve it. She had promised to remain silent, but as the women began to talk about their experiences of holding a college degree and navigating the One Stop, she felt compelled to speak. She stated,

And I know it has to sound very frustrating to you when it is happening to you, and you know what, eighteen years ago I was sitting where you were sitting. I was laid off in the first and only time in my life in the recession in 1992 and wound up collecting fifty-two weeks of unemployment, and I had a master's degree. And you know, it was very frustrating, and I knew the system and it was still a frustrating experience for me, but I know it doesn't do any good to say to you, the decision is made that if somebody has a bachelor's degree that they are not going to provide training.

I found this interruption in the focus group quite poignant. Almost immediately the women in the room felt someone was listening to them. In fact, our focus group slightly veered from my questionnaire protocol to an information session for several minutes. The women realized they had someone who could address some of their questions about the system, and perhaps more important, she was someone that had once been in their shoes.

It was not just workers with higher levels of education who were experiencing challenges; older workers who had decades of work experience also found that they had a difficult time in the recession. The unemployment rate for persons aged fifty-five years and older has increased sharply since the beginning of the recession in December 2007, with a record-high level of 7.2 percent in December 2009. While the unemployment rate among older workers is lower than that for their younger counterparts, older persons who are unemployed actually spend more time searching for work than younger groups. In February 2010, workers aged fifty-five years and older had an average duration of joblessness of 35.5 weeks, compared with 23.3 weeks for those aged sixteen to twenty-four years and 30.3 weeks for those aged twenty-five to fifty-four years. The longer duration of unemployment among older workers also is reflected in a higher proportion of the unemployed who have been jobless for extended periods. For example, nearly half (49.1 percent) of older jobseekers had been unemployed for twenty-seven weeks or longer in 2010 (after the official recession ended) as compared with 28.5 percent of workers aged sixteen to twenty-four years and 41.3 percent of workers aged twenty-five to fifty-four years.[40] These older workers found themselves at the One Stop Career Center. In one of the focus groups of women I ran, one woman shared her concerns:

It is like me, I have been working thirty-seven years since I came to this country. I have never collected a dime on unemployment. So now I say, "Wow, you are fifty-eight and now you are going to unemployment and you are going to school." And that is a challenge, but I am willing to learn something new. I might improve my skills until it takes me to retirement, maybe I can keep a little part-time going here or there doing something I like. Like I said, thirty-seven years of work and now BANG, you don't have a job. It is very weird, and I don't know what to do with myself.

Years of dedicated work experience did not shelter individuals from being laid off, nor did this increase their chances of finding success via the One Stop Career Centers. In fact, age and tenure in a job actually tended to work against a client. These factors may lead to placement in seminars for workers who would have additional barriers to finding employment. In the seminar I attended that was directed at the "hard to employ," by my guess, at least half of the clients appeared over fifty years old—leading me to assume age is a factor in one's employability. The face of one client in that class stays with me to this day. He was an older man, perhaps in his early seventies, and he wore a three-piece suit to the seminar. Although he looked out of place, he sat in the front of the room, and he listened intently, taking copious notes on a legal pad. I did not have a chance to talk with him or get his backstory, but the image of him just struck me so profoundly. The challenges of older workers seemed to spark an incredible emotional response, from both the focus groups I conducted with unemployed workers and those with the One Stop Career Center staff. Perhaps it was out of concern for their future or their sorrow in the American Dream and social contract that did not seem to be fulfilled for them. Perhaps it reflects a broader economic anxiety that we all have about our retirement and work. What lies at its root may not be clear, but the ability of the system to address their needs in our existing labor market is quite a challenge.

The Emotional Toll of One Stop Visits

Jobs and job training are actually only part of the experience of the One Stop Career Center. As I was conducting my research, two main themes emerged from the clients—clients feeling "lost in the system" and the dehumanization process clients often endure. This was something that transcended the skills and educational attainment of the clients. Detailing and understanding their emotional experiences makes it possible to further tease out the larger implications for clients' long-term prospects for economic security and social citizenship, particularly in the economically vulnerable time of a "Great Recession."

There are examples of women I spoke with who had very positive experiences, and these experiences helped them to better define and work toward career goals. One woman noted,

The One Stop, I think they were very helpful, they did their best to explain everything to you, the testing that you went through. Mine is more of a career change then continuing in what I did before. They kind of pointed out a lot of options that were out there, and to me it was basically, I didn't have those skills to do now what I want to do. . . . So they were very helpful in the direction they pointed me in and kind of gave me more of a direction for what skills I needed to develop and where to go.

Another client noted that she needed guidance for training programs, and the counselor was very helpful.

I know when I went there and I had randomly picked these schools and not knowing exactly what I needed and what I should be learning. They were helpful in that. Finding a program of study that included what I wanted to learn. In fact, even when I came here and met with Joan, she really actually changed something around for me. She thought I would be better suited where she put me.

Another woman shared the experiences she had in one of the resume writing classes she took—noting not only that the woman was substantively helpful to the writing of her resume, but also that she followed up with her and helped correct her resume after she revised it.

I forgot the lovely lady's name that did the resume class with me, but she offered all of us her email and to send the resumes to her. She corrected mine and helped me out a lot. I thought she was very kind.

What was a common theme throughout the experiences of the women who had positive interactions was the opportunity to develop a career plan and understand the pathway to achieve it. There were treated fairly, as full persons and citizens. Their own nervousness or anxiety about their current situation was not completely erased by the staff, but redirected into productive career searching. However, when that guidance is not available, the women feel lost and helpless. Several women reported being lost, and in focus groups with me pleaded for guidance:

Please have the workers work more with the people who come in because I used to cry leaving because it seemed everyone was expecting so much of me and I was lost and I went in and I told you I was lost. Just think about it, I go into a room and I tell you I am lost and I have these two little children that are looking at me, help me.

In every session I attended, I had to fill out mounds of paperwork—often filling out the same information numerous times. The many forms and protocols the women had to perform often served to intensify that feeling. As one woman noted,

Paperwork is like totally overwhelming to me. Little stuff like that, and sometimes I don't think the counselors are ready to take some people who are saying, "Take me by the hand, please."

Tied to being lost in the system is the feeling that one has lost their personhood. Some women reported that they felt they were not treated with respect.

Everyone that I have dealt with at the actual unemployment office themselves, horrible. I mean, I worked for thirty years, and it doesn't matter what kind of mood you're in or they are in, you should still treat people with respect, and that man was the worst. And the girl downstairs, when you don't get a check and you need to find out why you don't get a check, same thing. They will not look at you eye to eye, they don't give you respect. They treat you like trash, and I know I am not the only one here that feels that way.

This is particularly troubling, as unemployment and workforce development services are not entitlement programs. As I noted earlier, they are insurance programs that workers have paid into and services that they supported. However, when they go to use the services they feel quite stigmatized. One woman shared with me that she would often wonder how her case manager could have a job when she did not. And, she further noted, how different the One Stop Career Center experience would be if she held the job of case manager there.

But what is the standard of someone having that job where they are going to sit back and look at somebody's resume and kind of analyze what kind of training they need and what their career options are, like, how do you get it? But I said, if they fire her and her boss came in and said this is the worst I have ever seen and if they fired her and gave me that job, people will be coming out of here exuberant and excited with new opportunities and information. I said, "How the hell is this woman doing this job?" She looked like a mess. She didn't present herself professionally. She didn't speak professionally. Well, she went over to talk to somebody, I stole a bunch of documents and literature off of her . . . she had big piles of opportunities literature.

Another woman relayed how she felt deflated going through the process of accessing services. For instance,

I went into that situation, looking for this training and this education and really gung-ho and excited. I waited for probably an hour to see somebody. I met with this woman for literally ten minutes, and I left depressed, angry, absolutely furiously angry that this woman had a job at all.

Others pointed out the contradictions of what they were supposed to do and the obstacles they faced trying to accomplish it.

"You are supposed to be participating in the One Stop training. You are not eligible to go to school." She stone-walled me in every direction. She did not seem knowledgeable. She could not give me any information on grants, loans, anything of the sort.

The feeling of being lost in a system while also losing one's personhood was clear to me the day I attended an orientation for clients whom the state unemployment office profiled as "hard to employ" and "likely to exhaust their unemployment benefits." This class was the most emotionally draining session for me as a researcher—you could feel the clients' nervousness and desperation in the room. When I attended that class early one summer morning, I was surprised at how crowded it was—so much so that the class had to be delayed for twenty minutes so that they could bring in another instructor. I had a hard time finding a seat, but finally found a middle seat between two other women. While we were waiting, the women around me were talking. I asked them how long they thought this would take—one woman who seemed to be somewhat knowledgeable in the area said that this was to "learn how to be unemployed successfully!" and that "we should be out in an hour." Another woman suggested I look at the windows in the room, and in particular how dirty they were. She then sighed as she concluded that she thought they could give someone a job cleaning the windows. We then spent the next two hours filling out forms, with little substantive information provided. And the information that *was* provided was sometimes not even up to date. For example, they provided a screen shot of the state's website on labor market information. It was advertising the "Summer Jobs Program for 2008." The problem was—this was the summer of 2009.

However, there was hope among the clients. One thing that demonstrated this hope was how much clients wanted to help each other. In one of the focus groups we were talking about the Supplemental Nutrition Assistance Program (SNAP), more commonly referred to as "food stamps," and the process of getting into it. SNAP is a critical public assistance program that helps provide food support for families. During the focus group one woman reported that food stamps would have made a big difference in her economic security, but she could not qualify. As she stated,

I needed to get food stamps. I didn't have nice cars at the time, but I did have two vehicles, and they wrote them down and adjusted my income. They said it, they take that down, the car as your assets, and they basically tell you, well you could sell your car for food. They are saying you have to be down and out. Well I am.

One of the participants in the focus group, hearing this woman's experiences, made some suggestions to help alleviate her food insecurity.

I go to food pantries, and you guys know about Angel Food Ministries. Go to angelfoodministries.com, and you can purchase a box of food every month, and I think it is like in Surf Town. And it is once a month, you have to order the food by the end of the month, like the cutoff date for next month is right around now and you pick it up. You buy the basic, it is like $30 and it is a lot of food, and if you buy the basic for like $30, then you can also buy the supplement for like $15 or $20 or something like that.

Clients sharing information on the services available in the local community was something that occurred several times during my time at the One Stop Career Center. Perhaps most profound was a time when a client tried to help me find a job. In one seminar I attended, a man next to me asked me why I was there. I said I was looking for work as a waitress. He then gave me his wife's email address because she worked at the Olive Garden and he was sure they were hiring.

As I struggled to understand the clients' experiences in the workforce system, I saw individuals when they were at some of the most vulnerable points in their lives—when they did not know if they would be able to pay their rent or feed their children; when they had to make the hard decisions about their economic futures; when they had to give up health care and hope they would not get sick; when they felt like their personhood was taken away; and when they were scared. From these experiences I saw the hope and power that emerged when the clients were able to get intensive career counseling or better formulated pathways to economic security. Clients saw their lives differently and positively. There were success stories and clients who gained access to skills and jobs that they would not have had otherwise. Unfortunately, I also saw the tensions that arose—and that were felt by both the clients and workers—between the need for immediate employment and the need for career pathways to economically secure jobs. When those jobs are not plentiful, where does that leave the millions of unemployed? No one I spoke to talked about trying to stay on unemployment for the full duration of extended benefits. And although some individuals I interviewed did end up exhausting their unemployment benefits, that was not their goal when they filed for unemployment when they lost their jobs. They wanted to work—for both financial and psychological reasons—but the workforce system and the labor market were sometimes not able to match them with that work.

CHAPTER 2

On the Front Line During a Recession

The experiences of the clients navigating the workforce development system represent only part of the story. Each day many unemployed and underemployed clients depend on the workers who staff the front lines of One Stop Career Centers. It is these workers who are tasked with helping clients navigate a complicated system, serving as gatekeepers to jobs and training opportunities, and maybe providing an understanding and sympathetic ear in times of despair. It is then equally important to understand the experiences of the front-line workers who staff the One Stop centers, those who are responsible for the implementation of the Workforce Investment Act (WIA) on a daily basis.

Over the past decade there has been increased attention paid to the front-line workers in social services. Much of this attention emerged from studies of the 1996 welfare reform act, in which both theorists and practitioners have pointed to the problematic nature of the traditional dichotomy between policy formation and implementation. Although policy is formed at the highest levels of government, it is expected to be implemented by workers who are often at the lower rungs of the policy ladder—staffing the front lines of local government and nonprofit offices. If the goals of employment and training policy are to ensure that individuals who need jobs are placed in them, that they receive the training they need to qualify for jobs, or both, policy leaders need to develop policy that the front-line workers at the One Stop Career Centers throughout the nation can effectively implement. However, as much of the literature has emphasized, "the process of translating laws into practice amply illustrates the slippage that can occur between a policy goal articulated at the top and its realization at the bottom."[1] This slippage happens in the field during interactions between workers and clients, and it is at these moments that policy may be adapted, remade, or even disregarded. Scholars and practitioners have shed light on "the production of policy" at the point of contact between public service bureaucracies and their clients.[2] Workers like those in the One Stop Career Centers can become "street-level bureaucrats" who can determine the degree to which and manner in which the rules dictated by federal and state agencies are enacted.

Studies have demonstrated how formal rules developed in Congress and state legislatures were, at times, misunderstood or even ignored by workers when talking to clients. Workers had to make choices regarding what rules to follow or which to highlight with different clients. And, as welfare offices remain underfunded, it is often difficult for workers to mandate services or monitor client behavior with limited resources.[3] One of the more interesting findings of this scholarship is that when legislators cannot resolve their differences in drafting law, the implementation of that policy in the field becomes the context for resolving any resulting conflicts and ambiguities.[4]

In the workforce system, like other social services systems, front-line workers shoulder a great deal of responsibility. They are often expected to make judgments and determinations that have an impact on individuals' and families' lives. They can provide a lifeline to an unemployed worker by helping him or her gain access to a training program or receive supports to allow him or her to put food on the table. They also must deal with the tensions and the emotion work that is involved in helping clients find jobs in an economy in which jobs are often scarce. In trying to accomplish this work, they themselves are working in environments that are characterized by low pay, heavy workloads, and lack of advancement. And unstable funding for workforce development creates tensions and contributes to high turnover among workers.

Studying this workforce comes with a specific set of challenges, in part because of these occupational hurdles. There are no national data that reliably and accurately capture who employment and train-

ing workers are—making a composite difficult to compile. "The Department of Labor has five job classifications pertinent to welfare and
employment and each includes a wide variety of jobs and work settings.
To date, there has been no effort to standardize job functions or positions."[5] Throughout the country, and even within some states, different
One Stop Career Centers have different titles for their workers. In various One Stop centers, workers may be referred to as "job coaches," "employment specialists," "counselors," and even "case managers." This not
only creates confusion for researchers, it creates a great deal of confusion
for clients and workers, and also can limit the potential for developing
effective career ladders and advancement in the field.[6]

Despite the lack of consistency in their titles, there are core functions
the workers perform. For instance, they oversee a range of career and
basic-skills-assessment tests, counsel individuals about potential career
prospects, provide guidance on how to approach job searches, refer can-
didates to specific employers, and refer those in need of additional services to appropriate support services. A small number of workers service
special populations, such as veterans, while others will work with a variety of clients. Staff are also teachers and facilitators who spend portions of
their work weeks developing, organizing, and delivering group trainings
on resume preparation, interviewing skills, and networking. They may
also spend hours following up with clients to ensure they are in compli-
ance with the unemployment or assistance regulations, or may try to be
proactive to help them attain further training or better jobs. And as the
need to reach out to businesses becomes increasingly important at One
Stop Career Centers, many front-line workers may be connecting with
local employers to determine local labor market and specific job opportunities. While these core functions need to be performed, many workers
also have to complete other tasks as demand continues to increase.

That the muddling of staff titles and roles was a problem became
apparent when I started talking to the front-line workers after I did my
undercover work. Overwhelmingly, they reported that clients are often
confused about which staff they should see when they arrive, creating an
immediate hurdle when they come into a One Stop Career Center. The

workers noted that the bulk of the materials from the state unemployment office tell clients, "See a One Stop counselor." The reality is that clients often cannot get to a counselor unless they have gone through other levels of employment services. And not all clients need intensive services; some may just need an interviewer to help them gain access to job openings or someone to help them update a resume. Other workers also raised concerns about the "counselor" title, noting that with it comes the presumption that the worker will be delivering emotional or psychological services—something workers are neither trained for, nor expected to perform, according to the administration.

At once, these workers are earning their own wage and serving as counselors, policymakers, and administrators, thus making their perspective a key prerogative to understanding. In this chapter, I turn to the official state policy to show the role that front-line workers are *expected* to play in the state workforce system. Then I turn to my data on front-line workers in the workforce system to understand how the production of policy occurs in One Stop centers. In particular, I focus on working conditions—such as staffing levels, expectations, and skill needs as experienced by front-line workers, along with the emotional labor they perform and the toll that this work takes on them, which has only been heightened by the economic recession. I consider how the workers also develop and engage in conceptualizations of the clients they are serving, considering how this affects the delivery of services. In telling their stories, I point out the challenges and contexts that front-line workers believe to be constraints on successful job placement and how that squares with the action they take to help workers in their job search process. These insights reveal both policy slippage and modifications that sometimes make policy work.

On the Record

As with the bulk of jobs, there is an official script that workforce professionals are encouraged to follow. New Jersey, like all states, is mandated by the U.S. Department of Labor, Employment, and Training Association to develop a unified plan for its public workforce activities as part of the Workforce Investment Act. According to the state plan,

The vision of the One-Stop Career system is to provide comprehensive services in a seamless, integrated and efficient manner to both employers and job-seekers. The success of the One-Stop system lies in the quality of services delivered by knowledgeable and trained staff.[7]

It is quite clear that the front-line staffs of the One Stop Career Centers are held responsible for the success of the system—indicating that the labor process and work practices are critical, and, perhaps even more important, that it is the quality of the services and interactions that are key to success. A statement as explicit as the one in the state policy could lead one to believe that the job positions in the One Stop Career Centers would require that workers possess stringent qualifications, have continual professional development to meet changing client and labor market needs, and be compensated highly—as the success of the entire system lies in their work.

In fact, the starting national wage for "employment specialists" falls between $10 and $15 per hour—below Wider Opportunities for Women's (WOW's) baseline for economic security.[8] The median wage for social and human services assistants was $13.56 an hour.[9] The Anne E. Casey Foundation's 2003 analysis of human services workers estimated that there are approximately 500,000 front-line employment and training workers in the United States, earning an average salary of $30,800—and noted that social services jobs are consistently ranked among the five worst-paying professional jobs. In a Public/Private Ventures study of Philadelphia and Houston workforce centers, workers similarly found salaries that ranged from $28,000 to $48,000 in each city. In that study, they did note that the higher salaries were found in larger private organizations, as opposed to public and nonprofit centers, as these workers were sometimes eligible for bonuses—usually based on set performance targets for client placement and retention—that could add up to $4,000 to annual salaries.[10] However, even including this potential bonus in their annual income, these workers were still not earning economic security wages. Very quickly into my investigation of front-line workers I began to see a significant irony—the workers charged with the responsibility of ensuring that unemployed and underemployed workers were prepared for jobs that offer economic security often do not have that same security in their own jobs. This irony is supported by an analysis—based on data from the U.S. Census Bureau's Current Population Survey—which found that, nationally, a significant slice of the individuals working in the nonprofit sector faced one or more barriers to employment, such as receiving public assistance or needing to attend a GED class.[11] As you can imagine, this wage also drives the type of employees that the One Stop can attract.

The job requirements for employment as a front-line staff member were equally surprising, given their stated responsibility for success. Employers were looking for workers who had a valid driver's license and a high school degree, although some employers did prefer to hire workers who had additional education or experience. The U.S. Bureau of Labor Statistics (BLS) goes on to note that without additional education, advancement opportunities are limited. However, even with advanced education, exactly what those career pathways look like is a bit unclear. And despite the official policy insistence that the workers are critical to the success of workforce policy, there are no federal requirements for training this workforce. This means that workers in a One Stop Career Center in New Jersey, or anywhere in the nation, may not be trained in ways similar to workers in another center in another state. And even within states there may not be uniform training protocols.

Of course, this raises an immediate red flag in regard to the implementation of policy. If workers are expected to meet performance measures set by federal and state entities, but those entities are not mandated to provide training to those workers, the chances of those policy goals being achieved become dubious. This is particularly troubling under the WIA, as the establishment of One Stop centers led to a coordination of services that requires front-line staff to serve clients with various backgrounds, whereas prior to One Stop centers, front-line staff typically concentrated on a single program area and saw clients with similar barriers. So even many long-time One Stop staff members may not have the sufficient experience to make informed decisions for clients participating in the wide variety of programs offered, and they often have few tools at their disposal to help with that decision work.[12]

Despite (or perhaps as a result of) the low pay and lack of uniform qualification and training requirements, the employment of social and human service assistants is expected to grow by 28 percent from 2010 to 2020, faster than the average for all occupations. As the BLS notes, "There should be good job prospects, as low pay and heavy workloads cause many workers to leave this occupation."[13]

While the official mandate is very clear on the role of the front-line worker, it somewhat obscures the role and the lived experiences of the client. The official plan reinforces the concept that the One Stop Career Center flow is not about the customers navigating throughout the system as an independent actor, but instead about the services delivered— the implication being that the worker is actually navigating the clients, directing them to appropriate services for their needs. For instance,

[The workforce systems] detail a sequence of services, not a customer flow. This allows for optimal flexibility in the delivery of services to meet the individual needs of all customers. . . . Value-added benefits from the initial interaction with the individual ensure success and use of the system.[14]

In this official directive, the idea is that the worker has the latitude to work with the client to individualize her or his job search needs. Indeed, such a statement seems to be encouraging discretion and leeway from the workers. Again, the guidelines note that the "value added" of the workforce system directly comes from the interaction that the client has with the front-line worker. The official mandate continues to stress personal touch and customer service. For instance, it is through the orientation and registration process that the role of the worker becomes quite important in the envisioned policy of the workforce system. A client may enter the One Stop system through a number of avenues—locating services online; walking in for basic information; receiving a referral from an unemployment office, a community-based organization, or a training program; or learning about services from a workforce staff member who is assigned to their place of employment as the result of a mass layoff or through the welfare system. But once they get in, it is then up to the workers to help them navigate the system. In the official state plan, the guidelines of the orientation session for the client are clear:

Initial orientation to the One-Stop system will take place by providing general information and distributing a customer Bill of Rights to every individual. This will clearly state the levels and quality of service that the customer can expect from the One-Stop system. Scheduling of other services may also occur at this level.[15]

In addition, "General information will be asked of the customers to first assess their needs and then direct them to the most appropriate service."[16] And again, the role of the front-line worker is held as the key to the success of the customer at this early stage:

Due to the level of information provided and the importance of this initial stage of assessment, the person performing the registration and orientation tasks must be highly trained and possess superior communication and assessment skills.[17]

This section of the official guidelines highlights two important points. First, it details exactly what this "value added" of front-line workers is: in-depth career counseling to those in the process of a job change, those desiring additional skills, those recently laid off, or those who have been historically unable to sustain employment. In addition, the front-line staff are responsible for referring clients to specific activities or support services that are needed to address additional barriers to employment that may be impeding the customer from obtaining or sustaining employment. Examples of such barriers are care-giving responsibilities or physical disabilities. This includes assisting clients in gaining access to agencies that provide additional services, such as rehabilitative services, child care, transportation assistance, or mental health services. Finally, workers may also do continual follow-up on all delivered services by ensuring that referrals are met and services are delivered. This is done through a variety of customer satisfaction surveys and data-collection methods, which are often the responsibility of the front-line worker.

Second, this section begins to explain what requirements are expected of workers. It states that they should be highly trained in communication and assessment skills. However, as noted, the federal policy does not provide those training guidelines nor funding, so it is up to the state to provide and find that training for workers. In New Jersey, the Garden State Employment and Training Association provides professional development via an institute that the association created. And much training that is available comes from national sources such as Dynamic Works, an online provider that has created a national certification to anchor the training, along with Global Career Development Facilitators and the Certified Workforce Development Professional. These for-profit initiatives often partner with state agencies to deliver training to front-line workers. While they may fill the gap in the policy, the lack of a coordinated training system means that the professional development is delivered ad hoc and without uniform standards.

Regardless of training or titles, many front-line workers often find themselves performing case management functions, something that is encouraged in the official policy. Case management in its broadest sense ensures the comprehensive transmission of information at every stage of interaction with the One Stop Career Center system. Ideally, this process begins with the individual's initial one-on-one assessment, during which a client profile is created. The worker makes the determination if the client needs to be referred to intensive services. Case management may also include the development of a plan for long-term intensive services or a reassessment of employment strategies. This includes an action plan with any counseling and additional services that are required to meet barriers. Of course, good case management, like the other responsibilities of the staff, requires extensive training and also the resources and time in the workday to be able to devote to the client.

Aware of the federal policy goals of the workforce system and the state's policy and plan for its front-line workers, I was curious to see how the workers actually implemented this policy. Was there slippage, like there is in welfare reform? Were they able to serve as navigators for their clients as they move through the system? And how did they try to achieve the goals of the policy in the midst of one of the deepest recessions in United States history?

In the Field

Right off the bat, the workers told me they were at the One Stop Career Center to help the clients get a job. Yet the scope of what they needed to help clients with seemed larger than what the policy goals stated. In a focus group, one woman immediately said,

On my first day here my boss told me, "Suzanne, you are going to sit in front of someone and treat them with the best customer service you can because that's your job." That has stuck with me and anyone that I have worked with the same way. We might not always be able to give them the exact answers or things that they really want, but you really, really try to give them encouragement; something like the light at the end of the tunnel or something positive to leave this place with.

Her statement was immediately followed by a good deal of agreement from the other staff members. This worker and her colleagues understood that while the policy goal of workforce development policy is employment, the reality is that that goal cannot always be met. Imagine being this employee and on your first day learning that while you are here to help people gain employment, the real task you need to perform is customer service—helping people survive a tough time in their lives. Hearing this certainly frames one's work outlook—that one cannot always provide clients with exact answers or what they may think they want, but one can provide an environment that is supportive and encouraging. Regardless of the economy or the prospects for their clients, that is something that these workers can deliver on.

Workers did note that job placement was a critical goal, but they found that the work of performing emotional labor in the field often took precedence. This indicates a slippage in terms of the immediate policy goal of employment and training. Even if they could not meet the performance measures that were mandated by the WIA—the official policy aim—workers considered it a success if they made a difference in a client's emotional state. This also points to an interesting and innovative internalization of the state's plan by the worker. While the state may see the value added of the worker as navigating the system with the client, so that he or she can access services to achieve the policy goal, the workers see their value added as being the supportive and encouraging platform for the client. The human element of this work is a theme that continued throughout my discussions with workers. However, as will be seen, success was defined in the moment when they were serving the client, and not over prolonged counseling. As workers noted, it was important to give the clients something positive for them to leave their meeting with that day. In most cases, the workers felt that was the best they could do. And as the clients pointed out in the previous chapter, this was not enough. They wanted long-term guidance and resources, along with access to jobs. What the workers felt was sometimes the best they could do given the constraints of the policy and labor market, clients at some points experienced as a "brush off." Instead, clients wanted the workers to offer them some pathway to address their challenges.

Perhaps most noteworthy is that despite the official policy's stress on the interactions and intensive counseling provided by front-line workers, and the customer service that the workers know that they need to perform, these workers reported that this ideal is often far from the reality. All the workers I spoke with knew that they needed to help clients get jobs and that they needed to do so quickly. However, the focus on getting individuals quickly into jobs led many workers to report that they did not have the tools to meet the needs of their clients. This challenge was exacerbated during the recession, as greater numbers and more diverse clients came to the door of the One Stop Career Center. The WIA requires that program success be measured by employment, earnings, job retention, and knowledge or skill attainment. Front-line workers reported that the need to process through clients makes it very difficult to provide in-depth and individualized attention. As one counselor said,

We each see probably at least ten to fifteen people for assessment a day, and that is just to start. After that you got your testing and workshop and your assessment again and settled for school.

Breaking down this worker's statement in terms of her workday is actually quite instructive. Assuming an eight-hour workday and taking an hour for lunch and three hours for other job functions (such as group workshops, testing, paperwork, and so on), that leaves four hours per day to see clients. If one is seeing ten to fifteen clients per day, that leaves about fifteen to twenty minutes per client. Knowing all the responsibilities that need to occur in that meeting to help clients achieve the goal of job placement, that time period is quite daunting.

In response to the recession and with the financial support provided by the American Recovery and Reinvestment Act of 2009, the One Stop Career Center I studied did hire more workers, as the numbers of individuals needing assistance was amplified during the recession, yet workers were aware that they were still not able to meet the need.

We actually hired three new counselors to help us out because with the funding we wouldn't have been able to process enough people, we just wouldn't have been able to see them. We don't want them to have to wait and burn up their unemployment hours. We try to do things as quickly as possible. We hear stories of people having to wait months to get in and see someone, and that is just using up their unemployment time so we really don't like that to happen.

Still, they could not meet the demand from clients. As noted earlier, employment and training policy is strongly performance-based. Workers are asked to meet specific quantitative targets, resulting in many regarding their work as a numbers game. This creates a tension between needing to process clients and trying to get them placed into jobs or programs quickly, versus fully assessing their needs and the barriers that they may face. Listening to the workers talk about these challenges led me to reflect on the classes that I attended as a client. In each, the instructor told us that as soon as we did get a job—be it through the One Stop Career Center or on our own—we were to call the One Stop offices so that they could make note of it, and take us off the client list. It did not matter who we told the news to when we called, just that we should get the information to the local office. Hearing this in the class was a bit confusing, because it was preceded by the instructor holding up a blue postcard and telling us that we needed to send this postcard form to the state unemployment office in Trenton immediately when we found employment. According to state policy and practice, it was then the state unemployment office staff's responsibility to deliver that news to the local One Stop Career Center staff. So having to call the local One Stop office was an extra step for the client. Sitting in the class and hearing the instructor tell me this led me to feel as though the workers just saw each client as a number that they had to serve, and that they wanted us off their lists. However, hearing the workers explain this process put a human face on that decision. The workers told me that it could take weeks for the unemployment office to let them know when a client received a job. The time spent trying to follow up with the client was time taken away from the other clients they could serve. Therefore, they developed this local workaround practice with the intent of better serving all clients.

The workers reported that they felt very bad, and even guilty, when they could not give clients the time they needed, or could not follow the clients through the process. Indeed, one of their greatest disappointments with their work was that they could not always achieve what the official policy wanted them to do—navigate the client through the sequence of services to best meet their needs. Instead, clients often met with different staff members for classes, counseling, and job development—but typically did not have one staff member who could serve as their navigator. Often clients had lots of questions and needs, and setting boundaries that would allow them to simply process their workload could be difficult. As one worker noted, "Everyone that sits down in front of you wants all of your time." She went on to tell me that she often had to cut clients short or just work on an aspect of the barriers to employment the client faced, such as updating a resume, as opposed to trying to get a more comprehensive picture of the client's job search needs and challenges.

So much of the work was immediate triaging of clients to move them out of the shock phase of job dislocation. As a worker described,

Many people at that point, at the filing process, are into shock. You see a lot of people that come for those reemployment orientations that are like this. You could be telling them that they are winning the lottery and you just have to sign this piece of paper. It would go right over their head, because they are dealing with that loss, confusion, and where do I go from here.

Despite the burden of heavy caseloads and immediate client needs, workers tried to be creative in meeting the needs of clients, especially those needs that required a more holistic and comprehensive approach. One front-line worker shared the experiences of a co-worker who put together an extensive workshop for clients, particularly as a response to clients not being sure in which direction to turn. What is interesting here is that the workers acknowledge that, much of the time, the clients need more than an updated resume or a primer on interviewing skills; they need broader career counseling and advice. The creation of this workshop, initiated by the workers, was a clear attempt to meet the need of broader career advising in the context of heavy caseloads. If the workers could not meet this need on an individual basis, maybe they could do so in a group. As the front-line worker explained,

She runs a workshop and I do the substitute workshop, one of the things that she does in the workshop is a career focus. She talks about the different salaries you can earn, and she shows them where you can find out all that data online. She does a quick online assessment just to give them an idea of what an online assessment can do for you, so that they get an idea of all the variety of options that they have. She talks a lot about the transferrable skills and the alternate careers, not necessarily the field that we are in but where they can apply. Then she works with them on using the eligible provider list, the demand list. She shows them how to use all of that and salaries that you will be expecting to make if you took some types of training. A lot of the clients who go to the workshop come in thinking that they have an idea of what they want, and after they go through the workshop and realize what the job itself really is, they change their mind. Of course a lot of them don't have a focus at all; they are all just like, "I don't know what to do."

Another way that the workers tried to be more comprehensive guides was to try to use personal relationships in different units of the workforce and human services system to facilitate their clients' process, something that they are not required to do. For instance, maintaining unemployment benefits is critical to a client's economic security while unemployed. Staff reported how they would try to intervene in the unemployment offices when "something happens to their check." As one worker noted,

People talk about their problems with unemployment. That is the other thing. Unemployment is a big, big, big, big issue, and we try . . . because we have personal relationships. We make phone calls for people to try to help solve their issues with unemployment, but that is only because they used to work in our building and they know us so we can call them directly. But that is a big problem.

While workers had to make referrals to other services, the official work involved in that required the worker filling out a referral slip for the client. Yet the workers noted that a referral could take weeks to process through the system, and this wait time could have drastic impacts on the client. They also made it clear that many times when they had to make referrals for child care, transportation, or other support services, it often was not enough just to provide the client with a referral slip. Instead they needed to call ahead to the office to try to facilitate the referral in as quick a manner as possible. They noted that of course the workers in these offices were often just as overburdened, but their concern that their clients would be waiting for too long for services overrode that. Making phone calls to try to smooth things over for clients when things do not go right or fast enough, especially with the unemployment office, adds to the workload as well.

Emotional Labor—Each Day, Every Day

The motivation to provide high-touch services and extras was not solely inspired by the workers' knowledge of the system and the need to facilitate the bureaucracy to ensure that things would proceed smoothly. While this was certainly part of the reasoning, it was clear in my conversations with front-line workers that the desire to help the client navigate the larger social services system came from the great deal of emotional work that was part of the job. The workers formed an emotional connection with the clients, and they derived satisfaction from helping them solve even one aspect of their situation. So while they might not have been able to immediately get them connected to a job, they could perhaps move the bureaucratic wheels quicker so that a client could get food stamps for her family. In part, this desire stems from seeing client after client in emotional despair. One front-line worker told me,

And when you can't feed your family, it is really terrible what we have to deal with sometimes on a daily basis because these individuals just don't know which way to turn and where they can go to get the quickest training to get back into the workforce.

This was reiterated by another who simply said, "And some of the stories are really hard. It drains you by the end of the day."

Knowing the challenges that these individuals were facing, the workers reported that if there was something they could do to help the process, they felt morally obliged to do it. One worker shared the daily battle they faced:

But within the last two years, it really is emotionally draining. I have found that it is sometimes very hard to hold back tears, which I know is very unprofessional. But some of these stories are very hard to hear. These people are losing everything they have ever worked for in their entire life, and it could be any one of us at any given time and it is just sometimes very difficult to deal with. We try our best to do as much as we can and at least give them some direction from the moment they walk in, so they are not floundering and saying, "Is there any hope?"

Many of the workers felt an emotional tie to the clients they were seeing in their offices each day. Some of them told me that they knew many of them from their local communities, and that it was particularly hard to keep their emotions in check when their neighbors came to them in their most desperate times. Front-line workers also reported that it was not just the clients they personally knew that moved them to perform additional emotional labor. They told me that clients who were older were among some of the more emotionally draining to serve.

Then you have the individuals who have lost their jobs after being with a company for many years, that have lost their jobs to younger women and just can't understand what they did wrong other then they didn't have a great set of boobs. And this is literally what they say. It is sad, very sad. I had one woman who was employed with a company twenty-some years, and one day they said, that's it, you are done. She was replaced by two very young attractive women and knows that is why she was replaced. Those things are really devastating, very difficult. But we encourage from the moment they sit before us that there is light at the end of the tunnel, and that is the best you can do.

Perhaps one of the most powerful stories was shared by a front-line worker who met with a ninety-two-year-old woman who came to her looking for a job because she had outlived her savings.

My heart broke out, really. I had to hold myself back because I actually thought that was going to be me. I told her about [a counselor] and our program for fifty-five plus. I gave her a list of nursing homes because I said it might be a comfort zone for her. Maybe she could just answer phones, because she said that she used to work for Verizon. I gave her my cell phone number to get in touch with me to let me know how she made out. That was three months ago, and I haven't heard back from her. I don't know if she did get a job or if she changed her mind.

All too often the workers reported that they could relate to the clients, and that they themselves could just as easily be in their situation.

That is one of the most difficult parts of my job. I love my job, except there is a rapid response when there is a lay off. We go on-site and help them with the paperwork and explain all the available resources for them. I look at the faces of these people that are in my age bracket, and I know that they are not going to find a job making. . . . There was a delivery company, and they were making a really great salary, and they were not eligible for retirement. They were just right under the border of sixty years old, and to look at their faces and see the desperation. It is hard to deal with. It is hard to separate from.

The front-line workers had a front row seat in many cases to observe the clients' downward fall. When clients were facing economic despair, front-line workers were often left feeling sad and not able to provide them with the resources they needed to regain their economic security. In fact, one front-line worker told me,

There is no job security anymore. Nobody can be assured of their own jobs and achieving that level of economic security. This is the new normal. Our staff recognizes this, and our clients know this when they enter the front door.

So when they see clients on the downward spiral, they feel their emotional pain. As one woman told me,

And some of them were doing very, very well, and unfortunately in this country we all live above our needs, and you take somebody who was making $120,000 a year and then bringing him down to $50,000, he is still losing everything he has ever, ever had because it is not enough to make his monthly. So it is very difficult.

Other front-line workers pointed to a gender dynamic at play. As noted earlier, this recession, like previous recessions, hit predominantly male sectors of the economy hard, with significant job losses in construction, manufacturing and trade, transportation and utilities, and administrative and waste services.[18] The predominantly female front-line workforce had to deal with an added component to their services—more men coming into the One Stop Career Center.

I mean you have men that come in, and they have worked their whole lives and have good income, and they will be crying in front of you. And that is humiliating for them, and they don't even know what to do. They are at their wits' end. But we do have a lot of success stories, and that is what keeps you going. And you know what? It helps you too, because when you are thinking about the other client, when you are sitting in front of me, you say, "You are going to be okay." Because we know other people have been okay. You are not the only one that has ever been unemployed and you will be okay. I mean, you know, we were excited this summer, one of our summer kids got hired by a company off of work experience for a green job for $17 an hour. So you are like, "Wow, this is a kid who was going nowhere."

The work of performing encouragement and emotional labor is not something these workers were trained for, but something they and their supervisors identified was needed and that they try to figure out the best way of doing.

This is our own invention. This didn't come with a script. It changes. This is our own little . . . it grew out of the original beacon because people would come to us and they just didn't even know, their concepts were just not what were really going to happen. So this really grew out of that, and it has been evolving over the last three or four years now, and it changes according to the economy and so forth.

And when they could not meet the need with jobs or services, they turned to emotional supports that they could deliver. One worker noted that they had to do a great deal of self-confidence building.

Lots of encouragement from the moment they sit down. I mean, they will open up to you, and you will just encourage them to stay focused, and that there is,

I think, one of the biggest issues is age. A lot of women are afraid that because of their age they are not going to get hired, and you have to constantly reinforce that there are employers out there that do want the more mature worker and that will definitely give them a shot, but it takes a lot of encouragement.

And being the person who can calm down a client and help them deal with their current situation is increasingly important.

Just the other day this fellow was all agitated when he came in, and by the time he left he said, "Well, at least thanks for taking the time out to talk to me." They are not so panicky. This isn't the end of the world. You will work again. We may just need some adjustments along the way.

Yet the pressures wear on the front-line workers. They reported burnout and emotional exhaustion. One worker told me how she responded to these challenges:

We eat. . . . I don't want to talk to anybody when I get home, because you get to the point where it is really very draining. You know I surely do not want to talk on the phone when I get home, I don't.

The increased pressures and stresses on the front-line workers have been felt throughout the country. In a series of focus groups with staff and supervisors that I conducted nationally with my colleagues at WOW, overwhelmingly, supervisors reported that front-line workers face significant emotional stress in their work, and that especially over the past few years the workforce system was inundated with increased numbers of clients, many of whom were unemployed for several months or years and facing economic ruin. Workers and managers reported the need for resources that would help front-line workers cope with and overcome the stress and psychological and emotional toll their work inflicted. Yet burnout and stress discussions and services are more commonplace for other social services workers—such as child welfare workers and social workers. Over the past decades, researchers have documented secondary traumatic stress (STS) disorder—when professionals who repeatedly are exposed to the trauma of others begin to experience the symptoms of stress disorders. STS is defined as "the natural, predictable, treatable, and preventable unwanted consequence of working with suffering people, that is, the cost of caring."[19] In these examples, the workers experience the negative effects of trauma that are almost identical to the primary effects.[20] Particular focus of the literature has been on the effect of trauma work on social workers in settings dealing with family violence,[21] child protective service,[22] sexual abuse,[23] and grief and loss.[24] In all cases, STS is an occupational hazard of the job. However, STS frameworks and treatments have not been readily applied to workforce center workers. My study of the workers on the front line of the economic crisis suggests that better understanding is needed of the emotional impact of this work on the worker.

The counselors felt that they tried very hard to help everyone and often had to work around the policy regulations to accomplish their work. Interestingly, despite the increased workloads and performance measures, they attempted to do exactly what the official policy wanted them to do—be the value added to the clients as they are processed through the system. As one woman said,

See, one thing here, all of our counselors do everything, so everybody gets kind of the same treatment. I always say funding is just a bookkeeping issue. The client is the client and you know, whatever that person needs, it doesn't matter what the funding is.

And in the end, the counselors agreed that perhaps the best they could do was this:

You try to do what is best for them to keep them going so they get their benefits and make it as palpable as possible.

Social Structures and Individual Choices

Serving on the front lines during one of the nation's deepest recessions in modern history also provided the opportunities for workers to reflect on the impacts of social structures on their clients' opportunities for success. Each day, the workers were aware of the unemployment rate in the state and also aware of what jobs were available. In fact, the front-line workers were quick to identify the challenges of the economy and social structures. The United States labor market is changing, and it is not surprising that the front-line workers at One Stops are keenly aware of these changes. During the recession, employment losses occurred throughout the economy but were concentrated in mid-wage occupations. Yet during the recovery, employment gains have been concentrated in lower-wage occupations, which grew 2.7 times as fast as mid-wage and higher-wage occupations. The lower-wage occupations that grew the most during the recovery include retail salespersons, food preparation workers, laborers and freight workers, waiters and waitresses, personal and home care aides, and office clerks and customer representatives.[25] So workers spend a great deal of time trying to serve clients in an economy that is producing jobs that will not offer them economic security. As one worker noted,

There are many challenges at this point in time with this depressed economy. The direction in which we have always tried to steer them before is somewhat tainted by the economy. There really is very little direction that we can say for sure they will get a job, and before we could do that.

Another quite graphically laid out the situation from her experience at a job fair in the local mall that she had participated in the week before. At that job fair the majority of jobs were retail work paying minimum wage or slightly above, and rarely provided employment benefits.

Last week I had ten people waiting to see me. One by one, looking for full-time jobs with medical benefits and pays more than $9 an hour. That's just not prevalent around here now. So, you tell them to go to a Plan B or Plan C, if you have to.

The lack of jobs that offer wages that provide economic security was one of the biggest challenges front-line workers felt they faced in working with clients, and this was directly related to the social structure in their minds. This was graphically illustrated at a focus group meeting my colleagues at WOW and I held in 2012 with twenty-six front-line workers throughout New Jersey. We had the opportunity to get their feedback on integrating an economic security framework into their workforce services. We shared Table 2.1 with them, which illustrates the Basic Economic Security Tables (BEST) for different family types in New Jersey and asked the workers what their reaction was to it and if

TABLE 2.1. Basic Economic Security Tables (BEST), 2012*

Monthly Expenses		New Jersey, Selected Family Types			
	One Worker	One Worker, One Infant	One Worker, One Preschooler, One Schoolchild	Two Workers	Two Workers, One Preschooler, One Schoolchild
Housing	$940	$1,103	$1,103	$940	$1,103
Utilities	$166	$195	$195	$166	$195
Food	$279	$399	$603	$511	$807
Transportation	$707	$796	$796	$1,298	$1,400
Child Care	$0	$737	$1,426	$0	$1,426
Personal and Household Items	$347	$426	$477	$406	$528
Health Care	$151	$274	$451	$309	$506
Emergency Savings	$100	$144	$182	$133	$214
Retirement Savings	$119	$119	$119	$128	$128
Taxes	$588	$841	$1,096	$651	$1,221
Tax Credits	–$5	–$138	–$267	–$5	–$267
Monthly Total (per Worker)	$3,392	$4,896	$6,181	$2,269	$3,631
Annual Total	$40,704	$58,752	$74,172	$54,444	$87,132
Hourly Wage (per Worker)	$19.27	$27.82	$35.12	$12.89	$20.63
Additional Asset-Building Savings					
Children's Higher Education	$0	$136	$272	$0	$272
Homeownership	$404	$312	$312	$404	$312

Notes: * Workers with employment-based benefits. "Benefits" include unemployment insurance and employment-based health insurance and retirement plans.

Source: Mary Gatta and Matt Unrath, "Measuring Economic Security in the United States." Presentation at the Garden State Employment and Training Association Conference, Atlantic City, New Jersey, 2012.

they would share those numbers with their clients. Front-line workers reported that it confirmed the trends that they saw in the field. Each day, the workers were aware of the unemployment rate in the state and also aware of what jobs relevant to their education and skill level were available. They were also fully aware of the demands from both job seekers and the workforce system to ensure immediate job placement. The BEST table defined for them the daunting task they faced in responding to and managing client expectations and income needs.

The front-line workers were not incorrect in their assessment of the jobs available in New Jersey. Figure 2.1 benchmarks the wages individuals need to be economically secure in New Jersey, while showing the jobs with the largest projected growth. As is clear, the only growth job that offers economic security for families is as a registered nurse—a job that needs a good deal of education and training in order to qualify for entrance. All other jobs fall under the level of economic security for all family types.

As a veteran worker summed up, these changes she has seen over the past decades were quite significant in her ability to serve clients.

It's stressful. You know how things have changed in this county? Eighteen years ago when I first started I would be able to pick up that phone if I liked someone sitting at my desk and get that person a job. Now, I'm lucky when I pick up that phone that I can get that person an interview. That is how things have changed. But there is hope! What goes down comes back up! You have to think of hope.

In addition to noting the social structures, workers also emphasized that the clients did not come from cookie cutters, and that they had a diverse set of needs.

Every individual is different based upon the needs, their experience. I mean we look at everything that entails what would lead them to success.

The front-line workers clearly recognized challenges for job placement and economic security because of child care, transportation, incarceration, and other barriers. Without question, the workers talked about child care as the significant barrier. And they saw it as something

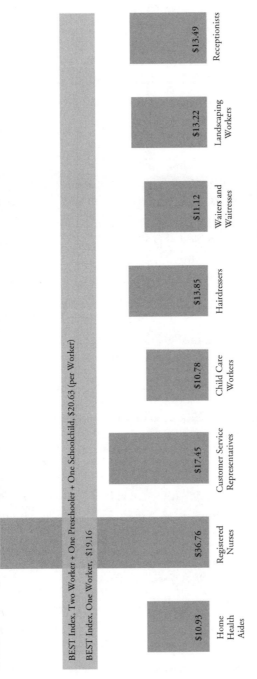

FIGURE 2.1. New Jersey Basic Economic Security Tables (BEST) versus average 2011 wages of selected New Jersey occupations with high projected growth through 2018

Notes: WOW and author's calculations from New Jersey Department of Labor and Workforce Development and U.S. Department of Labor, Bureau of Labor Statistics.

Occupations arranged in order of total openings due to growth.

Source: Mary Gatta and Matt Unrath, "Measuring Economic Security in the United States." Presentation at the Garden State Employment and Training Association Conference, Atlantic City, New Jersey, 2012.

very logistical—if the client could get affordable and local child care, they could solve a significant barrier.

That's just it, if this person is collecting unemployment, they have to be able to able, available, and actively seeking work. If they were offered a job, what would they do with this child?

Often clients face barriers with child care that prevent them from even attending a job interview. As a worker told me,

I had a woman come in yesterday with her young, maybe four-year-old, son. She was going to go ahead and see about this job and wanted to take her son with her to go to the application. I was like, you can't do that.

They also pointed out that many clients face a litany of barriers that have an impact on their job search. For instance,

It is always difficult if someone has been incarcerated. I mean, that is a barrier there. Finding employers or careers that will employ them, so that is always a challenge.

While the front-line workers were aware of the multiple barriers faced by workers and the changing labor market, they reverted back to individual choices and personal responsibility as the determining factors for the client to secure the job. Most commonly, they noted that many clients would come in passive and expect the One Stop Career Center to have the jobs waiting. As one worker stated,

I think that the people that come in individually think that we have all these jobs and they can come in and we are going, "What do you want to do?" "Here are like fifteen jobs to choose from." I don't think they realize that it's not that easy. Or they come in and want us to do everything for them. In a lot of cases their unemployment is over and now they want a job. "I need a job today!" "What do you have?"

And even though they very much knew that the clients faced barriers, they still reported that the clients had to get over the barriers to get the job. In the area I studied, there was very little public transportation, yet workers made it clear that it was up to the client to figure out a way to travel to the jobs.

And they have to be realistic in how far they want to travel to gain employment. If someone says they are limited to up to five miles, we really have to go through what the possibility of that being is.

Perhaps this tension between social structure and individual choices is best put like this:

Within three weeks, they should have an assessment, be tested, and go into the workshop. Then it is up to them. They can go and look at schools and decide what they want to do. They got to get referred up to schools to see which ones they want to attend. So then it is up to them. If they don't come back quickly, that is their choice then.

The framing by front-line workers in this manner certainly is not unique to my research. Sharone dubbed this a process in which clients have to play the "diligence game" at One Stop Career Centers. On the basis of his fieldwork among blue-collar workers seeking job services at a One Stop Career Center, he found that in order to meet the performance measures set forth, staff must be selective as to which clients they direct services to, particularly focusing on clients whom the workers have a "sense" will succeed in finding employment. And the front-line workers identify this "sense" via the diligence game, in which clients, unbeknownst to them, must go through a series of invisible hoops to demonstrate their commitment to finding successful employment. The first invisible hoop Sharone identified occurred when the clients were attending the mandatory orientation classes. Here clients were told that there are guidance counselors who are available for drop-in consultations to discuss their situation. However, it was up to the job seeker to take the initiative to seek out one of the counselors—and if they did so, they had jumped through the first invisible hoop. Sharone further found that in those meetings with counselors, clients are further screened in terms of work history—with staff identifying clients who were recently laid off as good prospects to invest resources in, as they are more reliable and dedicated to work, in comparison with workers who have had frequent bouts of unemployment, longer unemployment durations, or both. As front-line workers further worked with clients, those clients that persistently took initiative and maintained follow-up with workers and services were simultaneously jumping through the invisible hoops and increasing their probability of receiving additional trainings and workforce services.[26]

The focus that front-line workers put on individual client "choice" and "initiative" is very informative in terms of the larger policy discourse. As in welfare agencies, particularly post welfare reform, a focus on individual choices and individual responsibility for one's success or failure in social support programs has implications for policy and practice. In welfare reform, "the emphasis on choice [affects] workers in two ways: it portrays the agency as fostering highly cherished values associated with freedom and citizenship, and it absolves the agency of responsibility for what happens to clients who choose not to cooperate."[27] In welfare reform, the choice rhetoric very much feeds into the ideological framework of poverty. Research in the field has well documented the fact that welfare reform policy suggests that clients are poor because they make bad choices—dropping out of school, using drugs and alcohol, becoming a teenage mother, and not working. This supported very individual explanations of poverty—that poverty is caused by the behaviors and choices of individuals and not by social and economic structures.

In workforce policy, especially as it is being practiced during the recession, it is a bit more difficult for workers to focus solely on individuals' choices as the reason for their current situation. Still, while acknowledging social structure, the One Stop staff reframed the discussion to the worker having to make choices and, more important, new choices, in light of the economy. For instance, one worker, clearly aware of the economic situation, framed the relationship between the individual client and the social structure as a "survival" situation.

I emphasized survival skills. This is a survival economy. You might not get what you want, but you have to figure out how to survive.

Interestingly, the idea that clients need to find some way to survive in the economy is also related, in part, to some front-line workers' perspectives on suggesting and recruiting women to nontraditional jobs. When I posed the question of whether they actively suggest nontraditional jobs and training for women, no one had an example of a time when they did. While they did not voice that they would discourage women from considering nontraditional work, they also did not suggest that they saw nontraditional jobs as a route to economic security for women. It simply was not on their radar screen. However, in the course of our conversation one worker noted the connection between nontraditional jobs for women and "taking any job that is available." As she stated,

How do women get to thinking about nontraditional jobs? Remind them that they need to be willing to do anything now to feed their families. Had a girl today who would work neck and neck with men.

In this example, nontraditional opportunities were not framed in the context that women would be able to access better-paying jobs or reduce occupation segregation. Instead, for this front-line worker, nontraditional jobs were just another way to stress that women need to take any job that is available to them in this labor market. Following on this point, another worker emphasized,

They have to be willing to do anything, again to feed their family. They have to be willing to do whatever it takes.

It was these statements about client choices that struck me the most in my conversations with front-line workers in the One Stop Career Center. Despite all that the workers knew about the labor market and the recession, in the end they felt that the clients had to accept the situation as is, and, perhaps even more startling, had to accept that they (the clients) might not be able to retain an economically secure life for themselves and their families. In light of the economic recession and the changing job market, front-line workers face the task of having to lower client expectations regarding prospective income in new jobs.[28]

The need to lower client expectations of potential incomes and jobs raises significant concerns. Indeed, the current economic context and the "on the ground" reality for workers set the stage for another point of slippage. Those with a front row seat to the devastation wrought by the "Great Recession" are under incredible stress to place job seekers in any job, let alone those paying $60,000 a year or with an obvious career pathway. This tension is particularly difficult for unemployed workers who had previously held a job offering a family-sustaining income. Front-line workers are forced to introduce these individuals to the supposed uncomfortable truth that such jobs are no longer available, and if they want work, they must lower their wage expectations. When I pressed managers and staff on this issue, they noted that indexes of economic security are quite accurate and important. However, they felt that in this climate it would be difficult for many of their clients to attain jobs that offer economic security. Further, in WOW's focus groups with staff at centers throughout the country, many managers reported that the front-line workers themselves are not earning what the indexes of economic security suggest they should, making it even more difficult for them to include larger discussion of economic security and social structures in conversations with clients. If many of these workers are not earning those wages themselves, how can they help clients (some of whom have fewer skills and less education) to achieve economically secure jobs?

This tension—helping clients better understand economic security and gain jobs that provide it, and workforce professionals seeing the need to lower client expectations regarding economic security—is a challenge that may be amplified in upcoming years. Further, this tension is supported and underscored by the front-line workers internalizing much of the personal responsibility rhetoric that we see in welfare reform.

Front-Line Workers—Policymakers?

Throughout my conversations and interactions with front-line workers in the field, I was interested in understanding if their lived experiences highlighted ways in which they were able to critique and adapt WIA policy in their offices—were they, in fact, the "policymakers" in the field? What became clear from my conversations was that front-line workers—who could not always meet the official goals of the One Stop Career Center—may not as much be adapting WIA policy as instead turning to three main strategies to help them deal with the tensions they were facing in the field. These strategies include providing emotional support and hope to clients, encouraging clients to lower the expectations about the available jobs and salaries that exist in the labor market, and instilling a sense of personal responsibility for their labor market success.

Both workforce policy and the labor market structures have shaped the front-line workers' labor processes and responses to the challenges of the recession. Anthropologist Sandra Morgen argued that for welfare workers, the policy changes that occurred as a result of welfare reform created a situation in which the public assistance workers were subjected to the effects of devolution and privatization in their everyday work while also becoming accomplices in promoting their policies to clients.[29] The workers I spoke with seemed to be caught in a similar bind. Workers were concerned about the increased wait times that clients endured in the unemployment system and the decreased levels of case management that they could provide. They were also very vocal about the reality of the low-wage labor market and the quality of jobs that were available to clients. And when they could, they would try to facilitate the process for clients in ways that could get them quicker access to services or supports.

However, similar to Morgen's analysis of welfare workers, the front-line workers in the One Stop Career Center did not appear to place their concerns and struggles with working within the workforce system into a larger critique of the policy guiding their work. Instead they seemed to embrace the individual responsibility mantra of the WIA. Instead of a critique of broader national and state jobs policy and how the growth of the low-wage workforce has made their jobs more challenging, they defined their role as being able to help clients *accept* the reality of the labor market. And they actively tried to help clients find ways to make that new reality work for their new reality—encouraging them to lower their own family budgets and find ways to cut costs. Yet when they tried to make sense of their own inability to consistently meet performance goals, they were quick to mention that the jobs were just not there to place individuals in. Here the labor market inefficiencies took center stage in their explanations. This is a very uneasy and contradictory picture that they painted of the labor market—the lack of available and good-quality jobs made it difficult for them to perform their work, while simultaneously that same labor market structure could not be an excuse for clients' inability to be reemployed. And this conflicting conceptualization of the labor market plays out the tensions that the workers face between what the workforce policy officially mandates and what they are able to do.

Yet how this tension is experienced by workers involves more than just focusing on individual strategies that the clients need to follow (that is, lower expectations or demonstrate responsibility). Coupled with this is that workers engaged in emotional labor with clients, along with finding ways to provide smaller acts of kindness that would help clients. Arlie Russell Hochschild argues that the emotional labor that service workers have to perform—via repetitive and structured scripts— has led to the distancing of a worker's "authentic self." She differentiated between deep and surface acting in interactive work. Deep acting refers to when an individual is not just expressing emotions externally but actually feels those emotions, while surface acting is when the individual outwardly expresses emotions without actually subjecting his or her feelings to those emotions.[30] The front-line workers very much engaged in deep-acting emotional labor. They felt the stress and despair of their clients, and those disturbing emotions stayed with them when they left their offices. Tied to the emotional labor was the interpersonal connection that they sometimes tried to make with their clients. And they took pride in the notion that if they could not help the client meet her or his job goals, they reverted back to what they felt they could do—some small act of kindness[31] in the time that they met with them. In many ways this was how they defined the "value added" of the official state record. While they may not have been remaking or critiquing the policy they were tasked to implement, they felt that in those moments they were able to adapt the official policy in such a way that they could leave the client with something. Yet while it may have been a way for them to reconcile the tensions of what they could actually do for the client, it was not always experienced that way by the client. As was made clear in Chapter 1, clients were frustrated by the lack of solid job leads or access to education resources. Of course, they wanted to be treated well and voiced concerns when they were not, but they very much wanted a route out of unemployment. It was that latter need that was harder for the workers to deliver on and also harder for them to challenge within the policy framework they faced.

CHAPTER 3

Understanding the Backstory of Workforce and Welfare Policy

The experiences of the clients and the front-line workers at the One Stop Career Centers during the economic recession were not only informed by the current economic crisis and job market but also carry with them many remnants of public workforce and welfare policy over the past century. First, one thing to stress is that federal funding levels for employment and training programs at the U.S. Department of Labor have consistently declined during the past century. After peaking in real terms in 1979 at about $17 billion, funding has declined since then. By 2003, inflation-adjusted funding had fallen by about 65 percent from its 1979 peak; by 2008, by nearly 70 percent. However, that decline is actually an underestimation. If one takes into account that the economy has more than doubled in size since 1979, this funding has fallen by about 87 percent in relative terms—from roughly 0.30 percent to 0.04 percent of Gross Domestic Product.[1] And just from the start of this century, adjusted for inflation, Workforce Investment Act (WIA) state grants have been cut by nearly 40 percent since 2002.[2] As the WIA has a mandate for universal services, more individuals are being served by employment and training programs today then were thirty years ago; therefore, the decline in spending on the most vulnerable job seekers has been even greater. So the workforce system, facing significant challenges, along with a deep recession and recovery, is receiving less funding to provide services than in the past.

Adequate funding is critical to a successful workforce system, and the declines in the past decades have been sorely felt in the field. However, this history of funding is only part of the story. Workforce policy today carries with it a history that shapes how workers and clients understand and experience the workforce system, along with often reproducing structural inequalities. To understand where things stand today, along with how to chart a course forward, it is important to know the history that came before.

From Job Creation to Job Training to Job Placement

The current public workforce system first emerged out of the economic challenges of the Great Depression. During the 1930s, President Roosevelt created a series of employment and training programs as part of the New Deal. Through programs including the Work Progress Administration, the Civilian Conservation Corps, National Youth Authority, and Civil Works Administration, hundreds of thousands of unemployed workers received targeted training to qualify for subsidized employment in the public sector. The focus of these programs was on job creation, with education and training as only a small part of the policy response. However, the implementation structure of the training programs was quite unique for the time. Specifically, as Shaw and her colleagues have noted, as a result of the Roosevelt Administration's distrust of the current educational system, the New Deal training programs were administered through community-based organizations.[3] In addition, the Wagner-Peyser Act of 1933 established the Employment Service, begun as an agency to refer the unemployed to extensive public works programs established under the New Deal.[4] Further, the Wagner-Peyser Act added resources so that the Employment Service could maintain an effective nationwide system of employment offices.

Historical accounts have also demonstrated that New Deal programs were implemented differently depending on the gender of the clients. New Deal employment and training programs had significant gender and racial biases. For instance, women's participation was limited to only one-sixth of program openings, and only "heads of households" received services. As a result, if a woman was married, she was excluded from services. In addition, these programs reproduced inequities that existed in the labor market by encouraging the placement of women in sex-segregated work and setting lower wage scales for women. The Work Progress Administration (WPA) reports justified these restrictions, citing "a desire to put some brake upon women's eagerness to be the family breadwinner, wage recipient, and controller of the family pocketbook" and "a desire to protect the WPA program against possible public criticism from employing too many women."[5] So right off the bat, many women were excluded from being "deserving" of the programs in the New Deal.

As the country entered World War II, the focus on the public workforce development system diminished, but quickly reemerged after the war via one of the country's most significant training programs—the GI Bill of 1944. This legislation provided returning veterans with tuition assistance and supportive services to attend college. As Shaw and her colleagues note, "this was perhaps the federal government's biggest intervention into education ever, and it opened doors to college for millions of MEN who otherwise would never have been able to afford it,"[6] as it was a program that disproportionally benefited men. Further, the Employment Service, under the Wagner-Peyser Act, was also modified after the war to focus on finding jobs for veterans and for those workers who were displaced by the transition. Instead of emphasizing universal access to employment services, the agency instead targeted veterans and civilian workers whose skills or age made it difficult for them to find work in the new economy.[7]

While the GI Bill was a policy intervention that focused on traditional post-secondary education as a route out of poverty, job training as an option became part of the policy response in 1962 with the Manpower Development Training Act (MDTA). Under the MDTA, recipients received short-term training courses (ten to fifteen weeks), to prepare them for entry-level jobs. And the Employment Service also moved beyond job matching to providing job training and an even broader array of human resource development services to disadvantaged workers.[8] Several years later the Work Incentive (WIN) program was created as a supplement to welfare policy (Aid to Families with Dependent Children, or AFDC). Under WIN, welfare recipients were provided with job training (along with a subset of recipients who were mandated into work). The GI Bill, the WIN program, and the MDTA were some indications that education and training were becoming a preferred solution to unemployment.[9] Yet as the MDTA was developed in large part to serve disadvantaged workers (for example, black workers and older women), and the WIN program was directed to welfare recipients, these workforce policies clearly fell within the "undeserving" camp.

In addition, the coupling of the MDTA and the WIN program also points to a significant historical moment that was beginning to take shape in federal workforce development policy: "education and training were soon reframed as a means through which to reduce welfare dependency, and work emerged as a legitimate component of welfare."[10] However, during this period education and training were still a relatively small aspect of the policy response, and when used were directed to low-skilled workers. Over the ensuing decades, training programs began to be matched with comprehensive public employment and services programs. Education professors W. Norton Grubb and Martin Lazerson traced the growth of "services" strategy in public workforce policy.[11] Education and training were part of a larger strategy—including supports such as child care, transportation, and Medicaid—to help individuals work their way out of poverty. A key milestone in this policy evolution was the passage of the Comprehensive Employment and Training Act (CETA) in 1973. The CETA was a public service job creation program that created unskilled and semi-skilled jobs and training for individuals to succeed in those jobs.[12] CETA programs were targeted to disadvantaged adults and youth, and, similar to the original New Deal employment programs, it was administered locally; states generally were not involved in the administrative structure. Again, similar to New Deal programs, community-based organizations were often responsible for the development and implementation of CETA programs. As political scientist Gordon Lafer has noted, these organizations were often aligned with the interests of the workers and not the employers. Accountability was measured by the number of people served, not on outcome performance measures, and no funding was tied to actual performance. Yet the CETA was quite successful in providing jobs for disadvantaged workers. "At its height in 1978, CETA had provided nearly three-quarters of a million jobs for adults, and an additional million summer jobs for teenagers."[13] While the CETA focused on public service job creation, education and training were seen as secondary, but important tools to reduce unemployment and poverty.[14]

However, as the country proceeded through the early 1980s, a policy shift was in full force that highlighted a more individualized conceptualization of poverty, along with the potential for "transformation through job training. The rising popularity of skills-building strategies served to undermine the support for public service jobs."[15] And here was the biggest shift, one that continues to have an impact on individuals today as they navigate the public workforce system. The problem of poverty was conceived not as a lack of jobs but as a lack of skills on the part of the worker. On the basis of that reasoning, job training, not job creation, was then seen as the appropriate policy response. In 1982 the United States took a new approach to employment policy—a move away from public jobs and a focus on training and skills building as the legitimate way to reduce poverty—and CETA was replaced by the Job Training Partnership Act (JTPA).[16]

The JTPA was enacted with a good deal of bipartisan support, and indeed was a radical realignment of the CETA, in response to specific concerns about how workforce services were structured and delivered.[17] First, the job creation of the CETA was eliminated, shifting the JTPA's focus from "directly alleviating poverty and employment toward providing the means through which individuals could rise out of poverty."[18] The JTPA had a focus on the poor, and eligibility for JTPA services was determined by a means test. In addition, budget authority was no longer at the local level, but instead given to the states. Implementation of training programs was moved away from community-based organizations and centralized in private industry councils—indicating a movement away from the worker as the "client" to the employer as the client. The goal became how to better serve employers in finding workers. Finally, 6 percent of JTPA funds were allocated to provide incentives to meet performance standards, setting the stage for a movement away from program implementation and toward program outcomes.[19] The JTPA was quite successful in providing training for low-income adults, although the evaluations of how well the training translated into jobs and increased earnings were less than impressive.[20]

Occurring alongside the skills policy arena were changes to welfare policy. In 1996 President Clinton signed the Personal Responsibility and Work Opportunities Reconciliation Act (PRWORA). This newly designed "work first" model of welfare removed any notion that welfare was a social entitlement and severely restricted access to education and skills training. The PRWORA's aid program, Temporary Assistance for Needy Families (TANF), set a two-year limit to find paid work and a five-year lifetime limit on the receipt of federally funded cash benefits by individuals. TANF was based on the idea that paid work was better than welfare, education, or job training. This reframing of poverty as one of "inadequate workforce attachment and dependency on govern-ment" led to a new workforce policy in which "the human capital no-tion at the root of JTPA was quickly replaced with a work-first idea that held rapid job placement and reduction of welfare rolls as its primary goals."[21] And even more so than in the JTPA, the definition of "client" continued to shift away from workers and toward employers.

In 1998, the JTPA was replaced with the Workforce Investment Act. Sharply departing from the country's history of job creation and educa-tion to address workforce needs, the WIA instead focused on short-term training for immediate placement in the private sector. To accomplish this, One Stop Career Centers—a mix of privately and publicly man-aged local agencies—were established across the country to organize delivery of workforce development programs under the responsibility of Workforce Investment Boards (WIBs). In this system, the WIBs—representing both the public and private sector—coordinate and oversee education and job training at the state and local levels.

The WIA works across federal, state, and local levels of government. At the federal level, Congress authorizes the Adult, Dislocated Worker and Youth funding programs via the WIA. This law establishes the workforce investment system, which authorizes state and local WIBs, requires state reports yearly, and sets forth performance measures. At the state level, WIBs are appointed by the governor and include representatives from business, labor unions, state workforce agencies, elected officials, community-based organizations, service delivery groups, and others. The state WIB is responsible for a strategic plan and oversight of the workforce system. While states are responsible for planning, the local area is responsible for the implementation of workforce delivery. This is accomplished through local area WIBs that oversee the local One Stop Career Centers and operators—the loci of the workforce system.

The data by gender that are available demonstrate that women are not particularly well served through the WIA. Center for American Progress policy analyst Liz Weiss, in her report on women and the WIA, found that in 2008 female WIA exiters in the Adult Program earned 71 percent of what male exiters earned after a year of services. She notes that this wage gap was actually worse than the national wage gap of 77 percent that year. In part, Weiss found that this was related to the type of occupational training women received via the workforce system. While women are about as likely as men to receive training, and actually more likely to receive training for longer than men, women are consistently trained for traditionally female, lower-paying occupations. She reported that the top occupations that women received training for in recent years were "nursing aides, orderlies and attendants," "licensed practical and licensed vocational nurses," "registered nurses," "medical assistants," and "office clerks." In contrast, the top five occupations that men were trained for were "truck drivers, heavy and tractor-trailer," "truck drivers, light or delivery services," "welders, cutters, and welder fitters," "production workers," and "electricians." Very few women were trained for nontraditional occupations—indeed only 1 percent of all adult women exiters, and 1 percent of all female dislocated worker exiters, entered nontraditional occupations for women after participating in a WIA program. Weiss pointed out that this percentage is lower than the labor market, in which 5.5 percent of women work in nontraditional jobs.[22] The data that highlight the gender differences demonstrate that the inequality that overtly surfaced in the New Deal programs almost a century earlier has become more subtly embedded in workforce policies today.

Low-Skilled Clients, Women, Welfare, and Workforce

Presenting myself as an unemployed waitress, I entered the One Stop Career Center on that cold spring day in a position similar to many of the clients. However, I knew that the policy environment had been progressively shifting away from promoting education and skills training, and instead was operating under a model of immediate job placement. The movement away from a policy of skills development over the past decades has led to countless low-skilled clients remaining in low-wage work, without access to the resources necessary to secure education and skills training needed to advance into higher-paid jobs. In fact, the preceding discussion of workforce policy over the past century is not complete without a companion discussion of welfare policy.

The past few decades have marked a pivotal turning point in social welfare history. Public discourse was dominated by fierce attacks on welfare in the 1990s, which led to the eventual passage of the PRWORA in 1996. The PRWORA was a significant piece of legislation that overhauled the U.S. welfare system by replacing AFDC with TANF, a time-limited system that requires recipients to participate in work or work-based activities in order to receive cash assistance. The 1996 law was publicized as "welfare reform," and President Bill Clinton promised to "end welfare as we know it." This has continued into the 2000s as welfare and workforce policies slide toward a position that puts low-wage clients, and in particular single mothers, into low-paying work and poverty.

We cannot understand the workforce system without recognizing the gendered and racialized history of welfare. Welfare policy is not new, but the changes and impact relative to women have evolved over a century. At the turn of the twentieth century, policies emerged as a way to provide a social safety net for single mothers. The government provided women with the economic supports that would allow them to survive without paid work and a man's salary. Based on societal fears that if single mothers went into the paid labor force there would be an increased number of delinquent children, and, perhaps even more important, fewer jobs for men, early welfare policy sought to keep single mothers out of the paid labor force under the guise of protecting children's upbringing. But the need to protect men's jobs cannot be understated as a key influencer. In turn-of-the-century America, there was a "shared sense of social order that accommodated job assignments by sex." In 1900, women constituted only 25 percent of the labor force. Within that group, most of the women were either immigrants or daughters of immigrants (40 percent) or African American (20 percent).[23] The most common job for immigrant women and women of color was domestic service; for white women, the likely posts were in factories and mills. To protect more desirable male jobs, public sentiment glorified the role of mother for women. "Skilled men often chose to defend their jobs and to rationalize women's labor by invoking the need for domestic comfort. They thus became partners to the domestic code, partners in reducing women's wages and shutting them out of work."[24] Theoretically, valuing women and caregiving actually restricted women's rights, and in particular the right to economic citizenship. Further, this served to divide single mothers; since the pensions were directed at widows, they carried a white middle-class moral imperative: women should stay home to take care of children. However, not all women should be home—women who were single mothers because they were unmarried, divorced, or deserted were not afforded such pensions. This led to racialized and classed notions of "deserving" mothers. For example, a 1913 report of the Massachusetts Commission on the Support of Dependent Minor Children of Widowed Mothers clearly indicated that widowed mothers were the deserving mothers. As the report stated,

By the Workman's Compensation Law aid is given to survivors upon certain fixed terms and without reference to the character of the recipients. The Commission believes, in regard to widows, that the best interest of the state could be more successfully served by a different disposition. . . . It believes that aid should be given only when there are young children in a good family and then only in respect to them. . . . Subsidy makes it feasible that children should stay with their worthy mothers in the most normal relations still possible when a father is removed by death. It is intended not primarily for those with least adequate incomes under the present system of aid, but for the fit and worthy poor.[25]

These distinctions continued to be amplified when the modern welfare state began with the enactment of the Social Security Act of 1935; the section of the Act that specified Aid to Dependent Families (ADC) did so "for the purpose of encouraging the care of dependent children in their own homes or in the homes of relatives . . . to help maintain and strengthen family life and to help such parents (usually mothers) or relatives to attain or retain capability for the maximum self-support and personal independence" (42 U.S.C.[601]). ADC was widely understood to be an extension of the "mother's pensions" or "widow's pensions" of the early 1900s.[26] There was no discussion of promoting work for women, or decreasing women's dependency on the state. Instead, the program was directly designed to raise the living standards of families who had become poor through no fault of their own (namely, the death of a husband).

With the passage of Survivors Insurance and Old Age Insurance in the 1939 amendment, widows were able to access these benefits, while unmarried, divorced, and deserted mothers were funneled onto ADC. This then, for the most part, moved widows from ADC to Social Security, and kept nonwidows on ADC. The 1939 amendment created a two-tiered unequal system of supports. Further, ADC payments were the only part of the Social Security act that was not considered an entitlement because the individual is in need. In addition, payments to those on ADC were often substantially less than to those on Social Security; were means tested, in which participants had to "prove" their lack of income and resources; were administered by the states, so there were not universal federal guidelines; and contained extensive behavior restrictions, including home visits (to make sure a man was not in the house) and periodic eligibility checks.[27]

By some accounts, the passage of the Social Security Act "led millions of women to become dependent on the most stigmatized and limited forms of public aid—Aid to Dependent Children (ADC)."[28] Based on the idea that the only women who deserved assistance were widowed mothers, not those who "chose" to bear children outside of marriage or were divorced or deserted, distinguishing among women became a critical part of this, and subsequent, policy discussions. In 1939, the Social Security Act was amended; widowed women who had been married to men who were covered by Old Age and Survivors Insurance (now SSSI) received coverage under it. These women and their children became part of a nationalized program with standardized benefits, albeit at a reduced rate. Yet other women were pushed off of Social Security and onto ADC—which now comprised mostly divorced, separated, unmarried poor, and nonwhite women. And ADC eligibility was altered to require documentation of extreme poverty as a condition of eligibility. The provision of benefits to the child only rendered mothers invisible. As a result, the program became increasingly stigmatized, and its beneficiaries were referred to as welfare recipients. No longer was there any remaining sense of motherhood as a service, nor support as a service-based entitlement.

As the marital status associated with single mothers changed over the century, so has the racial composition. Mothers' Pensions and the early ADC programs (pre-1939) were directed toward white middle-class widows. However, as this group of women made the transition to Social Security programs as a result of the 1939 amendment, single mothers who had few resources or little recourse other than ADC or AFDC replaced them. For example, African American women, many of whom had to move from the South to the North, as they were often displaced by the mechanization of farm work, found that they (and their partners) were ineligible for Social Security payments (as domestic and agricultural jobs were exempt from the Social Security Act).[29] They then only had one option left, to apply for ADC. Therefore, African American women and other women of color began to make up the bulk of ADC rolls.

By the middle of the twentieth century, a two-tiered system was firmly in place in the United States. "Respectable" white middle-class widows were able to access Social Security supports, and "undeserving" single mothers, often poor and of color, collected ADC. And no longer were payments to support the unpaid work of mothers; now the women receiving supports under ADC had to work outside the home. In fact, in the 1940s and 1950s many states forced women to work by lowering payments and restricting eligibility requirements of ADC.[30] Yet at the same time that poor women and women of color were being forced to work in the paid labor market, white middle-class women were being told that they should not work in the paid labor market. In fact, not only should white middle-class women not engage in paid labor, it was believed that if they did, it could easily lead to the destruction of their families and communities.[31]

So while poor mothers were being forced into the paid labor market, middle-class mothers were being forced out of it (or told not to enter at all). How did these two seemingly contradictory messages for women coexist? The answer is actually quite simple and is directly related to the need for cheap labor in an expanding United States service sector. Post–World War II, as middle-class women were told it was their "patriotic" duty to quit their jobs so that these would be available for returning soldiers, the growing number of service jobs, including jobs in child care, cleaning, cooking, and secretarial work, needed to be filled. Luckily for service sector industries there was a ready-made labor force. Many of these jobs would be performed predominantly by women of color, working-class women, and poor women who were either single or whose male partners could not financially support their families. Throughout the 1950s and 1960s, women collecting welfare were forced into paid work in the growing service sector, competing with poor and working-class women who were already in those jobs. The core result was the creation of service sector industries staffed by mostly working-class, poor, and minority women to provide forms of service labor to mostly white middle-class women.

The racialized and classed dimensions of these policies continued to be exaggerated in regard to work. Sociologists Frances Fox Piven and Richard Cloward, in their social history of welfare, cite numerous examples of "work first" programs in the middle part of the twentieth century that funneled poor women of color into low-wage work. For example, during hearings at the 1967 United States Commission on

Civil Rights in Jackson, Mississippi, it was unearthed that "welfare re-cipients in Mississippi's 'work experience' program . . . were assigned to private entrepreneurs who, according to testimony, were told to 'use them any way you can.' As a result, women were given 'work experi-ence' in dishwashing and heavy cleaning, in hauling gravel and cutting grass."[32] Further, in testimony before the same commission in Indiana one recipient, in response to the department's domestic service training program noted, "it seems rather unnecessary for a Negro to go to school to get a certificate to clean up someone else's home."[33]

The interplay of race, gender, and work was quite evident in the Southern states. Fox Piven and Cloward demonstrated that when ADC was implemented, many states enacted provisions that were designed to keep women of color (particularly black women) in the labor pool. For example, Louisiana in 1943 adopted the first "employable mother" rule requiring that if the mother was employable in the fields, the fam-ily would be denied AFDC payments.[34] Other states followed suit and made it clear that "any job was enough," a sentiment that persists today. So Georgia, in 1952, denied assistance to mothers who were deemed employable if suitable employment was available. Not only did suitable employment translate to any job at any wage, but Georgia rules compounded the issue by prohibiting welfare departments from supplementing that wage if it fell below the welfare grant levels. More-over, in order then to keep poor women and women of color in the labor force, they were also given less money than their white counter-parts. For example, in 1961 the median monthly payment to blacks was $24.40, while whites received $30.40.[35] While these practices were most prevalent in the South, they also were practiced in the North, resulting in the forcing of poor women of color into low-wage work throughout the country.

For about the next thirty years, recipients—98 percent of whom were women and disproportionately black—were forced to comply with local and regional cultural norms and workforce requirements. For ex-ample, states enacted "suitable home" rules or "man in the house" rules, and denied assistance to "employable mothers" (women with children who were no longer infants). Because each state could set its benefits level, this exacerbated inequities both within and between states.

By the 1980s, things had changed. The "new morality" focus of neo-conservatives sought a return to "traditional" families that supported women's participation in marriage, childbearing, and at-home work but not their movement into the labor market—unless they were poor and in need of financial support from the state. While poor women were the targets of new legislative welfare "reform" initiatives in both the 1980s and the 1990s, their participation in the Congressional and public debates was rebuffed and the complexities and difficulties of the dual roles of breadwinner and nurturer that they were expected to uphold ignored. Both conservative and New Right thinkers in the 1980s and the 1990s were also successful in creating and maintaining the image of a welfare recipient as a female person, most likely African American, often promiscuous, with many children, and willfully financially dependent on the state.

Indeed the image of the black welfare mother as the public face of poverty has allowed sociological concepts—namely differential access to economic opportunities such as high-wage, high-demand jobs; education; skills training; and health care—to be viewed as personal failings as opposed to the results of intersecting systems of inequality. A glaring example of this was the 1965 report on black families by New York Senator Daniel Patrick Moynihan. In that report, Moynihan contended that black economic progress had not been successful because of the high numbers of weak single-mother households among black families.[36] Such racialized conceptualizations of single mothers have allowed policymakers and others to mask the real causes of poverty: a lack of access to good-paying jobs for single mothers. As women rolled off welfare and typically into low-wage work, they had little opportunity to gain the skills and education to move out of these jobs and instead have remained in poverty.

And then while President Clinton was successful in "ending welfare," his administration's policy reform simultaneously rang in a disastrous new beginning in U.S. social history. When President Clinton signed the Personal Responsibility and Work Opportunities Reconciliation Act in 1996, it further "codified the view that welfare policy should reward and punish the intimate decisions and behaviors of poor single mothers."[37] The "work first" model of welfare removed any notion that welfare was a social entitlement and decreased opportunities to receive education and skills training. Participants had to work for their assistance, as PRWORA's assistance program Temporary Aid to Needy Families, was based the idea that paid work was better than welfare, education, or motherhood for this group of women. This stipulation forced welfare recipients into low-wage work and kept women funneled into traditionally female low-paying service jobs without the opportunity to improve their lives.

In the first decade of the twenty-first century, these women, along with other low-wage workers, often found themselves in precarious positions. They may have been stuck in low-wage work with reduced hours and incomes, or been unemployed without the skills or education to qualify for better-paying work in one of the nation's deepest economic recessions. Many of them found themselves entering the One Stop Career Centers throughout the country—sometimes as part of their requirements to qualify for unemployment insurance; at other times in the hope of finding information and resources that could help them move toward economic security; and in still others because they may have heard from a friend or family member that the One Stop could help them get a job. So they took the first step and walked through the door, and were joined by workers of various economic strata facing the economic recession as unemployed workers. They often had little knowledge that the system carried with it such a history.

And what they experienced was that many times, the workforce system was an extension of the welfare system—whether they had been part of that system or not. While some had positive experiences, often tied to front-line workers who helped them navigate the workforce system, others reported feeling lost and dehumanized. Some of them learned they were not "job ready" despite working in the past; others learned that the One Stop was not the place for them and were referred to employment agencies or their former college career centers. The highly bureau-cratized system lends itself to impersonal interactions that are often based on conceptions of women and work that are grounded in the historical implementation of workforce and welfare policy, and the inequities of the labor market. Yet when the system was most effective, both front-line workers and clients reported that its services were able to take into account the personal biography of the client and the structural factors of the labor market and workforce system.

CHAPTER 4

Charting a Course Forward

As I saw throughout this project, and as I hope to have conveyed in the foregoing pages, the workforce system carries with it a deep history of perceived and real challenges that have discouraged some individuals from accessing services and support, and that have significantly affected its ability to fully meet the needs of all workers. During the economic recessions, the positive and negative aspects of the system have been amplified, as larger and more diverse groups of individuals need services. In this final chapter, I first share some of the key findings that emerged from my research and the ways that local officials tried to address aspects of them in New Jersey. I then look ahead in order to lay out a broader agenda for change, based on what my time as an unemployed client and my conversations with women navigating the workforce development system can teach about workforce policy in the United States.

Key Findings

By digging deep into a One Stop Career Center, I was able to better understand the lived experiences of both clients and workers during the "Great Recession." One Stop Career Centers, which have existed for decades, face significant challenges in meeting the needs of the diverse clients who come through their doors. In part, this stems from a larger policy culture. The history of workforce development policy cannot be divorced from the history of welfare policy. Therefore, the mantra of individual responsibility for one's lot in life—even when structural constraints are being reported by the front-line workers in that system—remains the overriding narrative in which client experiences are couched. The women I spoke with reported very similar experiences to those that women in the welfare system have reported—blame for their situation; lack of self-motivation; dehumanization; and being held solely responsible for navigating the bureaucracy and their own fate in life—even after having been referred to the One Stop explicitly for assistance. A work-first mentality is paramount in the One Stop Career Center—even when jobs, and especially good jobs that offer economic security, are not plentiful.

And when clients then find themselves unable to secure a new job or just churning through the low-wage labor market, the dominant narrative becomes even louder. One must work harder in her job search, and she must change her expectations—meaning lower them—concerning what jobs she will take and how much income she will earn. This became clear in my time at the One Stop Career Center when highly educated women and women with years of work experience filtered through the workshops. Recall the woman who was laid off from her job as a pharmaceutical manager who was told that her hobby of sewing would provide her with an opportunity for work at a Michael's crafts store. When employment and training reflects the welfare discourse of individual responsibility and work first, it has not met the needs of clients who may be from the welfare rolls or the managerial suite. This persistent narrative even more clearly highlights the disconnect between the philosophy behind policy and the reality of women's lives.

Simultaneously, front-line workers are confronting this policy disconnect on a daily basis. They acknowledge that there are not enough good jobs (or even jobs) to place people in, and raise concerns about the economic futures of their clients. They report higher workloads and workplace stress in trying to complete their own jobs in this environment. Yet they do not seem to make the larger connections between their experiences in the field and the larger context of workforce policy and labor market structure. How can they stop to see this with the constant influx of new faces?

This leads to an even greater tension between the goals of workforce policy and the reality in the field, particularly in regard to job placement and access to education and training. Yet this tension is not just a result of ill-fitted philosophical underpinnings. As noted throughout my research, workforce development funding is shrinking, making opportunities for education and training—which is a route to economically secure jobs—increasingly less likely for clients. Workers and clients both saw the value in access to education and training to move into good jobs and support families; they just often lacked the resources to materialize that vision. Instead, front-line workers report that they spend time trying to lower the expectations of clients for their futures—not a good policy for these individuals or the America workforce at large. And recommending nontraditional jobs for women may only come up when such a job is available; this is not framed within a larger effort to bridge a gap or even understand the recruiting of women to new types of opportunities. Further, diminishing resources and increased numbers of clients also lead to significant challenges in providing in-depth career counseling, long-term intensive work with clients, and a deeper analysis of job skills and career pathways. Of course, part of this is consistent with clients' wishes: they need jobs now to pay rent and provide food for their families. In addition, front-line workers want to be able to place clients—it is a sign of success and often emotional relief. However, the question that remains is, What type of success is this? With the lived experiences inside the One Stop Career Centers exposed, what can make an impact on workforce policy and practices?

Some Changes at the One Stop Career Center

As I was completing my data collection, I did share my findings with local and state officials. My insider perspective in New Jersey and the commentary that I've shared with you here were met with much interest by the local and state officials. The local workforce system officials, including the Workforce Investment Board (WIB) coordinator, the One Stop operator, and county workforce leaders were very willing to learn from the study and to try to redesign workforce services if possible. Yet there were only a few issues that emerged from the research that they were able to tackle directly.

One of the first things local officials dealt with was the reemployment seminar I attended that lasted just a few short minutes. They worked with their staff to better structure the seminar so that it would be substantive and uniform, and would provide a clear overview of the services available. They developed up-to-date materials for clients and provided workers with training on the most effective ways to deliver that information. They also eliminated the reemployment seminar that was directed at the "hard to employ," consolidating all clients into one core track. This also allowed clients to attend just one reemployment seminar, with the hope that they would then move on to other services more quickly and with less repetition. In addition, the reemployment seminar was provided to clients in an online environment throughout the state.[1] This not only involved creating an online class but also allowed for the integration of the unemployment insurance system and the reemployment seminars. In practice this meant that when someone applied for unemployment insurance via the online unemployment system, he or she was automatically directed to an online reemployment seminar, which could be completed right then. This eliminated some of the waiting time between filing for unemployment insurance and taking a reemployment class. Anecdotal reports from the field find that this change is saving time for the clients and also freeing up additional worktime of front-line staff at the One Stop centers to provide more assessment and individualized case management for clients.

In addition to the reemployment seminars, one of the issues that came to light in my study was a lack of good data on which jobs are growing in number and what the qualifications were to prepare for these opportunities. As a result, a detailed labor market information class was developed that shared information on growing-in-demand jobs, qualifications, and career ladders for clients at all levels. Again, officials reorganized the teaching format in the seminars, in this case to make them more interactive and less lecture-driven. Networking and class introductions were part of all classes, not only for community building and practice, but also because clients might have contacts that can help other clients.

These changes mattered, yet as you read them here, they may seem pretty basic. Providing updated information to clients is important, and should be done. Clients should not have to arrange travel and child care only to be provided with a few minutes of a workshop and then told to "check out the website" for details. Follow-up plans should be provided at any interaction, not considered a luxury. On the other hand, however small these changes may be, they illustrate some of the needs that can easily get lost in a large bureaucratic system.

While my analysis was just a piece of the rethinking that was occurring at the local and state levels, I was interested to see how the clients and workers at local One Stops, having gone through the recession and the impending recovery, were experiencing the workforce services. I went back to my local contact in 2011 and asked if I could do a few follow-up focus groups. The women I met with were not the same women that I had interviewed during the recession, but they represented the same composite of low- and high-skilled workers. These focus groups involved significantly fewer clients than my earlier ethnographic work, so they should only be considered in order to get a flavor of the current experience; their responses are not a detailed evaluation of any of the changes at the One Stop Career Center.[2]

One difference that the women I talked with reported was that they appeared to be more quickly assessed and directed to counselors, other seminars, or both right after the reemployment seminar than the clients I spoke with earlier in my research. This can help to eliminate the some-times weeks of waiting time that previous clients reported to me and the front-line workers voiced concerns about. This was highlighted by one woman as she relayed her experiences; after a meeting with a front-line worker, she was immediately signed up for a resume class:

At one of my interviews with one of the counselors, she suggested that because I didn't have a resume and I wasn't really sure how to write it, to take a resume class. It was very informative. The teacher was very good, although I don't re-member his name. He explained everything about what you should have in your resume and what you shouldn't have, with fine points and fine tuning. It's been helpful.

The women I spoke with who had taken the new reemployment seminar noted that at the end of the seminar they received appointment dates and times with a counselor. For the majority of the women I spoke with, that appointment was scheduled within two weeks' time. It is also interesting to note that this small change—having a date for the next step—made a difference in the clients' perceptions of the workforce system. By having a plan of action, the women felt that the process was moving forward after the reemployment seminar, and they also reported that they had a better sense of the workforce system. This latter sentiment was not as universally reported, though, as a few of the women in my follow-up focus group felt that even after the reemployment seminar they still did not have a full sense of what the workforce system was to accomplish. And several women reported that they could have used a tour of the One Stop Career Center, instead of just hearing that there were computers, faxes, and counselors available.

Another change was an opportunity for professional development for the front-line workers. Local officials wanted workers to get a sense of what the clients were experiencing in the One Stop Career Center, so they implemented a unique program in which they had their front-line workers visit One Stop centers throughout the state. In this experiment, the front-line staff posed as clients in workforce centers and attended classes and seminars as they tried to navigate the system. The staff was anxious at first to undertake the training, but after they did their visits, they felt somewhat differently about their jobs.

When they returned from their visits, they reported many of the challenges clients had reported to me—difficulty in even finding the One Stop center, sessions that started late and did not provide substantive and up-to-date information, and missing or conflicting information from the sessions. As experts in the field, they were surprised how much information about state workforce services was not shared with clients—including labor market information, state websites, and other supports. They were so astounded by the withholding of the information that several of the workers felt compelled to privately tell clients after the seminars they attended about resources that could help them. They also reported that they felt stressed and anxious sitting in the seminars. Many of the seminars they attended had little interaction between clients and staff, and they just wanted to leave the class as quickly as possible. The staff members were able to take back to their jobs lived experiences they had had as secret shoppers and therefore were better able to serve clients in the field.

As part of this professional development process, the staff had debriefing sessions with an organizational development consultant to integrate their experiences in other One Stop Career Centers into the everyday practices of the One Stop they serve. Through this debriefing process they were able to clearly define their interactions with clients in quite tangible ways, including giving fair and impartial treatment to clients, providing clients with tools for their reemployment, identifying the needs of clients up front and working to satisfy them, providing effective job leads, and doing all of this before a client's unemployment benefits expired. Critical to achieving a high level of customer satisfaction, the staff had to better understand the expertise and knowledge they possess and how they disseminate that information to job seekers. They had to ensure that this information was consistent and accurate, and the procedures for clients were uniform, working toward seamless services that provide basic tools and skills.

These changes made some differences in the experiences of the clients and workers. In many ways they amplified the "value added" that the workers felt they provided and prided themselves on. It seems that that clients also saw some benefit in that value added, perhaps coupled with more interaction with staff members. But also, these follow-up focus groups occurred after the recession was officially over, so it is also plausible that the larger national discourse helped to provide some degree of hope to the clients. Yet the reality is that these changes did not innovate the workforce policy or inspire One Stop Career Centers to address the larger and deeper tensions the clients and workers reported: the ability of the workforce system to deliver on jobs that offer a route to economic security. Clients were still exhausting their unemployment benefits and the jobs that were available were often low-wage work. There were still too few resources available for training and education. Workforce funding budgets continued to be slashed. There remained large caseloads for workers and little time or funding for professional development of front-line workers. The crisis did not end. Nor could the roots of it really be addressed in the One Stop Career Centers.

Looking Forward: A New Social Contract

Many have noted a key aspect of workforce development—it must be flexible so that it can respond to labor market changes as easily and seamlessly as possible. And in doing so, it must embrace the lived experience of the clients desperate for an effective system. Clients need consistent and clear information, and they need to be able to receive that information without barriers from a bureaucracy that is at times extremely rigid and unforgiving. Further, the emotional and psychological nature of the client needs to be taken into account. In the interviews with clients, and in my participant observation, it is clear that entering a One Stop Career Center for unemployment services is humbling, sometimes embarrassing, and even scary. Staff members need to be trained in understanding the clients' perspective, to ensure that they treat clients with humanity. Professional development opportunities need to be more available for workers to improve customer service, along with their own workforce expertise. And the emotional needs of the front-line workers need to be addressed. It is often forgotten that the individuals serving the unemployed are experiencing stress and anxiety as they try to help them.

As noted, a diverse group of clients are accessing services at the One Stop Career Center. Unfortunately, the workforce system has not adapted the services to the diverse group as quickly as the demand needs, and tends to serve each client in the same manner, as if they are welfare-to-work clients. Customizing resources and plans to the diversity of clients who need them involves having money and time. It also requires a reframing of the career pathways that are available to clients and a real understanding of what education and skills people need at all the stops along the way to proceed along those pathways and work toward economic security. If the workforce system is to meet the needs of different groups of workers, it cannot be an either-or situation. There is a real caution here, as the workforce system needs to address the diverse groups that are in search of services, yet adapting services to higher-skilled workers should not be done at the expense of traditional clients (such as the welfare-to-work population). Similarly, the larger public, and not just the unemployed, should be made aware of and integrated into One Stop Career Center services. The use of seminars, mentoring programs, and social networking can help in this process. This will not only destigmatize the One Stop Career Center and its public association with "welfare," but also provide job resources and information to larger groups of people. In doing so, this can increase the reach and scope of the workforce system by expanding networks and potential employment connections for clients. Redesigning the physical space of the centers so that they resemble career centers and not government offices can help to change their image and also increase the comfort level of individuals and employers.

These changes and needs, though very much focused on the micro-level of the One Stop Career Center, emerged from the lived experience of workers and clients and can make a real difference. While these recommendations do make a difference in helping to improve workforce services, in and of themselves they are not enough. What is clear from the lived experiences of those who are part of the WIA is that improving the reality of workforce development is only half the battle; there must be jobs available that offer economic security that individuals can be placed in or for which they can receive training. Yet this promise is harder to materialize, especially in the current economic context, in which job growth is overwhelmingly located in low-paying industries. And the response of the workforce front-line workers to clients has been that expectations have to be lowered—the jobs that pay solid middle-class wages are disappearing and clients need to prepare for the new economic reality.

Economic development must be coordinated with workforce development. When high-paying jobs are not locally available, government policy should play a role in job creation, engaging the private sector in workforce development plans for the region. In addition, workforce systems can better integrate with agencies that provide income, housing, and child care supports, so that these benefits can close the gap for families with incomes that fall short of economic security. This is not too much to ask of government and industry if economic security is a national and regional priority, as it clearly is today.

Workforce development, human capital investment, and the overall picture of the American workforce are linked. In workforce development, the conversation needs to be about careers and career pathways, not just work. This is more than a semantic issue—there needs to be a real policy and cultural change in how policymakers formulate responses to the changing labor market and work trajectories in the various circles where conversations about these challenges are taking place. Right now, in the workforce development system, there is very little actual investment and development of workers in meaningful ways. And there is very little critique of this from inside the doors of the One Stop Career Center. Front-line workers accepted the work-first policy framework, knowing it had the real probability of not providing any real labor market routes to success for their clients. The WIA, even perhaps more so than welfare reform, has led to an internalization by front-line workers that since both clients and employers are to be served by workforce development systems, their role is to work with the clients to "whip [them] into shape so that they better meet the needs of employers and taxpayers in general."[3] This quite gendered and racialized belief has remained embedded in American welfare and workforce systems for many decades.

Of course, workforce system policies are not the only obstacles to connecting job seekers to beneficial long-term education or training programs. Individual job seekers need to pay bills and put food on the table. If they are interested in participating in training, they may want it to be the shortest training possible so that they can enter the workforce again quickly. Present economic insecurity, then, is a barrier to a worker's ability to build economic security over the long term, pointing to a larger issue of social supports when individuals are in transition. Moving away from a work-first framework allows for the full integration of education and training programs that are degree- and certificate-bearing for the long-term skillbuilding and educating of workers, so that individuals have the opportunities to advance in career pathways and qualify for new jobs.

However, one fact that was painfully obvious in my study was that the current labor market and projected occupational growth cannot be understated in discussions about workforce development policy. There are still many middle-skill and mid-wage jobs in the U.S. economy, and the workforce system can certainly still improve its practices to better connect clients to these careers.[4] These jobs, however, represent a decreasing share of the American labor market. In their stead, the economy is witnessing a significant increase in the share of low-wage work. The workforce system's prioritization of immediate job placement is not well-suited to the increasing bifurcation of the labor market.

Throughout this book, the backstory has been that the employment gains during the recovery have been highest in low-wage occupations. Jobs such as retail sales, food preparation, waiters and waitresses, and personal and home care aides grew 2.7 times as fast as mid-wage and higher-wage occupations. Overall, employment has grown by 8.7 percent in low-wage occupations compared with only 6.6 percent in high-wage occupations. And mid-wage occupations have actually fallen by 7.3 percent. This uneven jobs recovery means that the "good job" deficit is greater than it was during the early 2000s.[5] Further, the proliferation of low-wage work is compounded by decades of wage stagnation. Over the thirty years, the median wage for households has remained nearly the same.[6] Indeed, the past decade actually saw a decrease in the inflation-adjusted average income for households. Available wages and compensation for most workers remains far below what would be expected given productivity gains and what families require to keep up with increases in the cost of health care, housing, and education.[7]

Despite its name, low-wage work is not solely defined by inadequate pay. These jobs also are often characterized by the absence of other important workplace benefits, such as paid time off, savings programs, and health care. Even when health coverage is provided, low-wage workers pay a greater share of employment-based health care premiums than workers in higher-paying jobs—something that many cannot afford. Further, low-wage workers are less likely to have long-term disability insurance, short-term disability insurance, and access to life insurance, and are less likely to have pension coverage or other retirement plan options with employer contributions.

Also common among low-wage jobs is the lack of control that low-wage workers have over how, when, and where they work—some of the primary benefits of workplace flexibility. And ultimately, there is very little national legislation that is directed toward improving the ways workers can better address work and family demands. The Family Medical Leave Act (FMLA), which provides workers with a statutory right to up to twelve weeks of job-protected unpaid leave, is limited in its scope, covering only workers who meet certain requirements (such as working at large companies and having specific care requirements). Many low-wage workers do not meet the criteria, and even if they do, they cannot afford to take unpaid leave. Furthermore, companies that have fewer than fifty employees (about 28 percent of companies in the United States) are not required to comply with the FMLA.[8]

These trends in the labor market were not news to the front-line workers or the clients of the One Stop Career Center. It was something I heard over and over again, and it was a concern that led to a considerable amount of anxiety for both groups. The reality is that neither U.S. workforce development policy nor its jobs policy is able to address this issue as it stands now. Nor may it even be fair to place the need solely on workforce development policy. Central to this is that there needs to be a much larger policy reform—a new social contract. A significant aspect of this reform is that there needs to be a reconceptualization of poverty and unemployment away from individualistic frameworks. Researchers, politicians, and workforce officials alike know full well that few people choose to be poor and unemployed. In a country that praises and rewards success, achievement, accomplishment, and self-sufficiency, thinking that anyone would want to be regarded otherwise is absurd. Pathological, self-defeating behaviors and character defects are not primary causes of unemployment, and if they were, no amount of training, education, or behavioral remediation would alter them and the resources allocated to try would be wasted.

Moving away from individual explanations of unemployment is key to helping us move toward a deeper understanding of how education, workforce development, economic development, and public assistance can and must be part of the larger social contract. Economic security needs to be understood comprehensively to include aspects of several elements—income, job quality, education and training, savings and as-sets, and public supports.[9] So if the jobs that are projected to grow in number are low-quality jobs, how can these jobs be improved? Work-force development policy is certainly an important and critical part of this response, but for it to be an effective policy it cannot exist on its own. For this to occur, there needs to be collaboration between both private sector changes and public sector supports. For example, there needs to be an emphasis on high-road management practices—practices that engage front-line workers in problem solving and decision making and provide them with the training and skills to do this well—to im-prove the quality of service jobs and the quality of services provided. For instance, not all service jobs are the same, even within the same broad occupational category. Annette Berhardt, Policy Co-Director at the National Employment Law Project, noted that in retail work "markets for high-income customers or products requiring expert advice, multi-skilled, and better trained workers are required—they need to have the technical background to give advice, the soft skills to build relationships with customers, and the ability and knowledge to make decisions on their own."[10] For example, she notes that Home Depot workers earn significantly more than other retail workers, are typically employed full-time with benefits, and have significantly less job turnover. Moreover, since Home Depot employs a decentralized management, departments within the store are run autonomously, and hourly sales associates have considerable power to solve customers' problems and resolve customer complaints. In contrast, service jobs at mass discounters or fast-food restaurants are characterized by part-time work at low wages, along with increased levels of routinization and management control.

While higher-quality service jobs are not the norm, lessons from studies of management practices and work organization can be integral to the restructuring of these jobs in the future. In addition, it is necessary to unpack not only the nature of work organization but also the characteristics of workers. Even within the same occupations, lower-status service jobs are predominantly filled by lower-educated minority, immigrant, and female workers. As the service economy grows it can continue to bifurcate, with better jobs going to higher-status workers. Tied to this is the need to direct firms to move from low-cost, low-skills strategies to higher-value product markets in which higher skills are needed.[11]

Comparative analysis can prove to be very important not only in identifying high-road management practices but also in understanding the role of national labor-market institutions in improving service jobs. Economists Eileen Appelbaum and John Schmitt found significant differences in low-wage work in high-income countries. Specifically, when unions retain much of their traditional strength and influence, when employment regulations provide workers with protections against layoffs, or when a national minimum wage provides an effective floor that enables most workers to rise above the low-wage threshold, employers are less able to evade institutional constraints on their ability to lower wages and reduce employment security.[12]

In addition to high-road management, workers need benefits and supports to move toward economic security. However, whether workers and their families have access to health care, paid leave, flexible scheduling, and living wages are largely decisions left to employers. The absence of comprehensive social insurance or governmental protection results in a vastly unequal labor market, in which workers who fill low-wage jobs face many compounding issues. Significant policy reform which ensures that workers and their families have some level of basic economic security is unlikely to come in today's political climate, and so it is necessary to create pathways to the upper end of the labor market. Immediate job placement and an underfunded workforce system as answers to this challenge are starkly inadequate. Policymakers and advocates have more realistic expectations of the work and capacity of the workforce system, and an honest account of the realities facing workers and these programs points to appropriate policy and program responses.

It is critical to ensure that workforce development is on the forefront of this new social contract in order to address the challenges in the system, and to better serve women and their families particularly. Yet every year, workforce funding is subject to and often experiences budget cuts that force programs to do more with less—something that is impossible. And workforce development policy is almost always debated in the halls of Congress or in state legislatures in and of itself and not seen in its relationship to other policies such as minimum wage, health care, or social security. These policies must work together in order for any of them to be successful. If this can occur, than workforce development can be more about developing the workforce to truly meet the needs of clients and employers. Until then there will be individual success stories of unemployed clients, proactive workers, and even state programs that have made impacts. But real social change and improvement will remain elusive. And until this happens, it will be the clients of the system—and many times the most vulnerable of those clients—who will suffer the most.

Even after the recession, the unemployment rate for women who maintain families is higher than the national average, and the underemployment rate for workers with less than a high school degree has climbed. Millions of Americans who work full time cannot pay their basic living expenses, let alone have enough money to make investments in their future. These harsh realities demonstrate the need for reinforcing and expanding the safety net for working families facing hard times and supporting programs and policies that contribute to moving families to economic security, such as those contained within the workforce system.

Self-sufficiency for low-income, low-skilled workers often requires career pathways that lead to economically secure jobs, and in the economic recession the need for retraining many older, experienced, and educated workers into new fields became apparent. Improvements to the system are needed, along with adequate funding streams. It is my hope that those improvements not only will be grounded in sound outcome data from programs throughout the country, but also will include the lived experiences of the individuals who are in that system every day—the clients and workers whom I have been among and posed as one of in the eye-opening study that I have shared here. Policy is for the people. Starting policy evaluations with lived experiences and the realities of the labor market could help the system move to innovative and targeted solutions. When workforce development is grounded in the day to day, rather than viewed as a narrative about privilege, persistence, lack thereof, or political ideology, it can be aptly seen as part of a larger social contract that has as its goal economic security for workers, their families, and America at large.

Notes

Preface

1. For background on that project, see M. Gatta, *Not Just Getting By: The New Era of Flexible Workforce Development* (Lanham, MD: Lexington, 2005).

2. The focus groups and interviews were approved by the Rutgers University Institutional Review Board.

3. This additional research methodology was also approved by the Rutgers University Institutional Review Board.

Introduction

1. One Stop Career Centers are also interchangeably referred to throughout the country as One Stops, One-Stop Centers, Job Centers, Career Centers, and Workforce Offices, among others.

2. M. Szeltner, C. Van Horn, and C. Zukin, "Diminished Lives and Futures: A Portrait of America in the Great-Recession Era," a report of the John J. Heldrich Center for Workforce Development, Rutgers University, 2013, http://www.heldrich.rutgers.edu/sites/default/files/content/Work_Trends_February_2013.pdf, accessed September 9, 2013.

3. This estimate is based on data from the United States Department of Labor as of March 2013.

4. For good examples of a critical approach to workforce development policy, see, for example, K. Shaw, S. Goldrick-Rab, C. Mazzeo, and J. Jacobs, *Putting Poor People to Work: How the Work-First Idea Eroded College Access for the Poor* (New York: Russell Sage, 2006); J. Henrici, *Doing Without: Women and Work After Welfare Reform* (Tucson, AZ: University of Arizona Press, 2006); H. Holtzer, "Workforce Development as an Antipoverty Strategy: What Do We Know? What Should We Do?" Working paper #08-17, National Poverty Center, Ann Arbor, Michigan, 2008; and O. Sharone, *Job Searching, Unemployment and Self-Blame* (Chicago: University of Chicago Press, forthcoming).

5. The level of service a client receives will determine the amount of demographic data collected on that client at the local level. For instance, states are

not required to collect demographic data and create a client record for clients who use core self services. These individuals are then not captured in evaluations of the system, even though they make up a significant portion of the individuals receiving services.

6. These data are available from WIASRD (Workforce Investment Act Standard Record Data) via the U.S. Department of Labor, Employment & Training Administration website (http.www.doleta.gov).

7. A nontraditional job is one in which women make up 25 percent or less of the labor force.

8. One Stop Career Centers were piloted in the 1980s to bring together into one place employment and training services that work with all people, to make it easier for job seekers and employers to use these services. For a detailed discussion, see L. S. Jacobson, "Strengthening One-Stop Career Centers: Helping More Unemployed Workers Find Jobs and Build Skills," The Brookings Institute, 2009, http://www.brookings.edu/research/papers/2009/04/02-jobs-skills-jacobson, accessed September 9, 2013.

9. Core services are available at no cost to everyone. Individual One Stops determine how their core services are provided. An individual may receive core services as part of a large group, or service may be provided one to one. Some sample core services found at One Stop Career Centers include individual intake and orientations to services available; opportunities to better explore current and potential work skills; resource libraries or labs that provide access to computers, telephones, and fax and copy machines; online searches for jobs and training; access to job banks or listings of available jobs; free Internet access; resume development; job search skills training; networking skills workshops; interview techniques workshops; referral to an employer with current job openings; customer satisfaction follow-up; and determination of eligibility for additional services. For more detailed information on services provided, see S. Fesko, D. Hoff, and M. Jordan, "Tools for Inclusion: One-Stop Centers: A Guide for Job Seekers with Disabilities," Tools for Inclusion Series, Paper 16, Institute for Community Inclusion, ScholarWorks, University of Massachusetts Boston, 2000, http://scholarworks.umb.edu/ici_toolsforinclusion/16, accessed September 9, 2013.

10. Intensive services are available to individuals who are unable to obtain employment by using core services, and who meet specific eligibility criteria. Some sample intensive services include comprehensive assessments of skills and service needs; the development of an individual employment and career plan; customized screening and assessment; reference and background checks; intensive career counseling; in-depth interviewing skills development; computer workshops; one-to-one assistance with updating resumes, cover letters, and thank-you letters; and individualized case management. Referrals for training services may be available to individuals who have used core and intensive

services and have not become successfully employed, and who meet eligibility criteria. See Fesko, Hoff, and Jordan, "Tools for Inclusion," for more detailed information on services provided.

11. See Jacobson, "Strengthening One-Stop Career Centers," for a detailed discussion.

12. Ibid.

13. Ibid.

14. This is a point that will be taken up in greater detail in Chapter 3, particularly in how it affects the ability of front-line workers in One Stop Career Centers to serve the unemployed in ways that help them prepare for and gain access to jobs that can offer economic security.

15. A fuller tracing of history of the policy changes in workforce development since the New Deal is provided in Chapter 3.

16. Workforce Professionals Training Institute and Fiscal Policy Institute, "Deep in the Trenches: Understanding the Dynamics of New York City's Front Line Workforce Development Staff," 2012, http://workforceprofessionals .org/Deep%20in%20the%20Trenches%20Front%20Line%20Staff%20 Report%20Final.pdf, accessed September 9, 2013.

17. R. Jacobs, "Understanding Workforce Development: Definition, Conceptual Boundaries, and Future Perspectives." Paper presented at the International Conference on Technical and Vocational Education and Training, Winnipeg, Manitoba, 2002, p. 13.

18. National Governor's Association, "A Governor's Guide to Creating a 21st Century Workforce" (Washington, DC: National Governor's Association, 2002), 12.

19. For more information, see Jacobs, "Understanding Workforce Development," and Jacobson, "Strengthening One-Stop Career Centers."

20. K. Shaw and S. Rab, "Market Rhetoric Versus Reality in Policy and Practice: The Workforce Investment Act and Access to Community College Education and Training," *Annals of the American Academy of Political and Social Science* 586, 2003:172–193, at 188–189.

21. For instance, cash transfer programs such as food stamps or unemployment insurance are able to provide immediate benefits to clients.

22. N. Ridley and E. Kenefick, "Research Shows the Effectiveness of Workforce Programs: A Fresh Look at the Evidence." Center for Law and Social Policy report, 2011, http://www.clasp.org/admin/site/publications/files/work force-effectiveness.pdf, accessed September 9, 2013.

23. K. Magnuson, *Investing in the Adult Workforce: An Opportunity to Improve Children's Life Chances*, prepared for the Annie E. Casey Foundation Initiative on Investing in Workforce Development, 2007, http://www.aecf.org/ news/fes/dec2008/pdf/Magnuson.pdf, accessed September 9, 2013.

24. P. Harrington and A. Sum, "Workforce Development Challenges for

the Twenty-First Century." A report of the United States Conference of Mayors, 2002, pp. 10–11.

25. For a detailed discussion of emotional labor, see A. Hochschild, *The Managed Heart* (Berkeley: University of California Press, 1983).

26. H. J. Holtzer, *Funding for the Workforce Investment Act in Fiscal Year 2012 and Beyond.* Statement to House Ways and Means Committee, 2011, http://waysandmeans.house.gov/uploadedfiles/submission_2_holzer.pdf, accessed September 9, 2013.

27. J. Handler and Y. Hasenfeld, *Blame Welfare, Ignore Poverty and Inequality* (New York: Cambridge University Press, 2007)

28. Ibid.

29. E. N. Glenn, "From Servitude to Service Work: Historical Continuities in the Racial Division of Paid Reproduction Labor," *Signs* 18, 1992:1–43.

30. R. Sherman, *Class Acts: Service and Inequality in Luxury Hotels* (Berkeley: University of California Press, 2006), 49–50.

31. For more details, see R. M. Blank, "The Impact of the Recession on Women." Congressional Breakfast Briefing: Washington, DC, January 21, 2010, http://www.womenspolicy.org/site/DocServer/Rebecca_Blank_presenta tion.pdf?docID=2861, accessed September 9, 2013; and D. J. Besharov and D. M. Call, "Lessons from the 2008–2009 Recession: Response to Plotnick," *The Policy Studies Journal* 37, 2009, http://www.welfareacademy.org/pubs/pov erty/Besharov_Call_Lessons%20from%20the%202008-2009%20Recession -Response%20to%20Plotnick.pdf, accessed September 9, 2013.

32. Ibid.

33. H. Hartmann, A. English, and J. Hayes, "Women and Men's Employment and Unemployment in the Great Recession," Institute for Women's Policy Research briefing paper, 2010. p. 36, http://www.iwpr.org/publications/pubs/ women-and-men2019s-employment-and-unemployment-in-the-great-reces sion, accessed September 9, 2013.

34. Ibid, 33.

35. Wider Opportunities for Women, "Women's Work in 2011," 2012, http://www.wowonline.org/documents/TOP50OccupationsWomen2011.pdf, accessed September 9, 2013.

36. American Association of University Women, "The Simple Truth About the Gender Pay Gap: Fall 2013 Edition," 2013, http://www.aauw.org/ files/2013/03/The-Simple-Truth-Fall-2013.pdf.

37. P. Taylor, R. Kochhar, D. Dockterman, and S. Motel, "In Two Years of Economic Recovery, Women Lost Jobs, Men Found Them," Pew Research Center, 2011, http://pewsocialtrends.org/files/2011/07/Employment-by-Gender_ FINAL_7-6-11.pdf, accessed September 9, 2013.

38. Ibid.

39. For detailed case studies and analysis of the impact of education, see

V. Polakow, S. Butler, L. Deprez, and P. Kahn, *Shut Out: Low Income Mothers and Higher Education in Post-Welfare America* (New York: State University of New York Press, 2004); and Center for Women Policy Studies, "From Poverty to Self-Sufficiency: The Role of Postsecondary Education in Welfare Reform," 2002, http://www.centerwomenpolicy.org/pdfs/POV1.pdf, accessed September 9, 2013.

40. New Jersey Department of Labor and Workforce Development, *New Jersey's Unified Workforce Investment Plan: New Jersey's Talent Connection*, 2013, http://www.njsetc.net/njsetc/planning/unified/documents/NJ%20Unified%20Work force%20Investment%20Plan%202012-2017.pdf, accessed September 9, 2013.

41. Ibid.

42. See Ibid. for details.

43. M. Lipsky, *Street Level Bureaucracy: Dilemmas of the Individual in Public Service* (New York: Russell Sage Foundation, 1983).

44. E. Brodkin, "Street-Level Research: Policy at the Front Lines," in T. Corbett and M. C. Lennon (eds.), *Policy into Action: Implementation Research and Welfare Reform* (Washington, DC: Urban Institute Press, 2003), available at http://www.urban.org/pubs/policy.

45. S. Morgen, "The Agency of Welfare Workers: Negotiating Devolution, Privatization, and the Meaning of Self-Sufficiency," *American Anthropologist* 103, 2001:747–761, at 748.

46. N. Fraser, "Women, Welfare and the Politics of Need Interpretation," *Hypatia* 2, 1987:103–121.

47. Sharone, *Job Searching*, 4.

48. V. Lovell and C. Negrey, *Promoting Women's Workforce Security: Findings from IWPR Research on Unemployment Insurance and Job Training*, paper presented at America's Workforce Network Research Conference, Washington, DC, 2001, http://wdr.doleta.gov/conference/pdf/lovell.pdf, accessed March 1, 2011.

49. Ibid.

50. Ibid, 11.

51. L. Weiss, "Opening Doors: How to Make the Workforce Investment Act Work for Women," Center for American Progress, 2010, http://www.americanprogress.org/issues/women/report/2010/07/01/8165/opening-doors, accessed September 9, 2013.

52. As noted earlier in the chapter, women are concentrated in low-wage, traditionally female jobs and face a gender wage gap throughout the labor market. The workforce system can reproduce these inequities in job placement and training practices. This will be further illustrated in Chapter 3.

53. D. Smith, *The Everyday World as Problematic: A Feminist Sociology* (Boston: Northeastern Press, 1987), 19.

54. H. Gottfried and L. Reese, "Gender, Policy, Politics, and Work: Feminist Comparative and Transnational Research," *Review of Policy Research* 20, 2003:3–20, at 4.

55. Ibid., 4.

56. For a more detailed discussion, see P. Collins, *Black Feminist Thought: Knowledge, Consciousness and the Politics of Empowerment*, 2nd ed. (London: HarperCollins, 1999); and B. Dill, A. Jones-DeWeever, and S. Schram, "Racial, Ethnic and Gender Disparities in Access to Jobs, Education and Training Under Welfare Reform," presentation at the Consortium on Race, Gender and Ethnicity, College Park, Maryland, 2004.

57. While it is important to understand the racial differences among women, in my fieldwork I was unable to construct a sufficient sample size of nonwhite women that would allow me to draw sound conclusions. The county where I conducted my research was 91 percent white in 2010 (according to the 2010 U.S. Census Bureau). However, while I cannot draw out racial differences in my fieldwork data, I do supplement that data with discussions of other research that are able to do so.

58. S. Hays, *Flat Broke with Children: Women in the Age of Welfare Reform* (New York: Oxford University Press, 2003).

Chapter 1

1. U.S. Bureau of Labor Statistics, "Table 1.4: Occupations with the Most Job Growth, 2010 and Projected 2020," 2012, http://www.bls.gov/emp/ep_table_104.htm, accessed September 9, 2013.

2. Wider Opportunities for Women, "The Economic Security Scorecard: Policy and Security in the States," 2013, http://www.wowonline.org/wp-content/uploads/2013/05/WOW-Economic-Security-Scorecard-2013.pdf, accessed September 9, 2013.

3. Wider Opportunities for Women, "Living Below the Line: Economic Insecurity and America's Families," 2011, http://www.wowonline.org/WOW USBESTLivingBelowtheLine2011.pdf, accessed September 9, 2013.

4. Restaurant Opportunities Centers United, *Tipped Over the Edge: Gender Inequity in the Restaurant Industry*, 2012, http://rocunited.org/tipped-over-the-edge-gender-inequity-in-the-restaurant-industry, accessed September 9, 2013.

5. Some good examples are O. Sharone, *Job Searching, Unemployment and Self-Blame* (Chicago: University of Chicago Press, forthcoming); and D. J. Wright and L. M. Montiel, *Workforce System One-Stop Services for Public Assistance and Other Low-Income Populations: Lessons Learned in Selected States. A Report to the U.S. Department of Labor, Employment and Training Administration* (Albany, NY: Nelson A. Rockefeller Institute of Government, 2010).

6. C. J. Heinrich, P. Mueser, K. R. Troske, K. Jeon, and D. Kahvecioglu, "A Nonexperimental Evaluation of WIA Programs," in D. Besharov and P. Cottingham (eds.), *The Workforce Investment Act: Implementation Experiences and Evaluation Findings* (Kalamazoo, MI: W.E. Upjohn Institute, 2011), 33.

7. B. S. Barnow and C. T. King, "The Workforce Investment Act in Eight

States," a paper of the Nelson Rockefeller Institute of Government, 2005,. http://www.utexas.edu/research/cshr/pubs/pdf/Rockefeller_Institute_Final_Report2-10-05.pdf, accessed September 9, 2013.

8. Ibid, xvii.

9. D. Besharov and P. Cottingham (eds.), *The Workforce Investment Act: Implementation Experiences and Evaluation Findings* (Kalamazoo, MI: W.E. Upjohn Institute, 2011), 33.

10. Perhaps my reaction was a bit naive, but local banks and financial institutions in the area did not have uniformed security, so it was not immediately clear to me why the One Stop Career Center would.

11. R. Ghayad and W. Dickens, "What Can We Learn by Disaggregating the Unemployment-Vacancy Relationship?" Federal Reserve Bank of Boston Public Policy Brief, 2012, http://www.bostonfed.org/economic/ppb/2012/ppb123.pdf, accessed September 9, 2013.

12. As cited in M. O'Brien, "The Terrifying Reality of Long-Term Unemployment," *The Atlantic*, April 13, 2013, http://www.theatlantic.com/business/archive/2013/04/the-terrifying-reality-of-long-term-unemployment/274957, accessed September 9, 2013.

13. A. Jones-DeWeever, J. Petersen, and X. Song, *Before and After Welfare Reform: The Life and Well-Being of Low-Income Single Parent Families* (Washington, DC: Institute for Women's Policy Research, 2003).

14. A. Korteweg, "Welfare Reform and the Subject of the Working Mother: Get a Job, a Better Job, Then a Career," *Theory and Society*, 32, 2003:455–480, at 455.

15. Sharone, *Job Searching*.

16. C. Van Horn and H. Schaffner, *Winning the Workforce Challenge: A Report on New Jersey's Knowledge Economy* (New Brunswick, NJ: John J. Heldrich Center for Workforce Development, 2003).

17. B. Ehrenreich, *Bright-Sided: How the Relentless Promotion of Positive Thinking Has Undermined America* (New York: MacMillan, 2009).

18. Wider Opportunities for Women, "Women's Work in 2011," 2012, http://www.wowonline.org/documents/TOP50OccupationsWomen2011.pdf, accessed September 9, 2013.

19. This phenomenon is not found just in the United States. In the United Kingdom, for example, government agencies tasked with finding work for unemployed single mothers make the same assumption: with often years of isolation looking after their children solo, these women often lack good social skills. See D. Nickson, C. Warhurst, C. Lockyer, and E. Dutton, "Flexible Friends? Lone Parents and Retail Employment," *Employee Relations* 26, 2004(3):255–273.

20. J. Miller, F. Molina, L. Grossman, and S. Golonka, *Building Bridges to Self-Sufficiency: Improving Services for Low-Income Working Families* (New York: MDRC, 2004).

21. Many reasons account for this, including a work-first approach to WIA implementation, restrictive eligibility requirements for use of Individualized Training Accounts, and too little funding appropriated to infrastructure support. U.S. Department of Labor information reported in Chicago Jobs Council, "Improving Our Response to Work Needs: Recommendations for Reauthorization of the Workforce Investment Act of 1998," 2003, http://www.cjc.net/publications/files/2_Workforce_Investment_Act_PDFs/wia_improving_response_rpt.pdf (URL no longer active).

22. A. Frank and E. Minoff, "Declining Share of Adults Receiving Training Under WIA Are Low-Income or Disadvantaged," Center for Law and Social Policy, 2005, http://clasp.org/publications/decline_in_wia_training.pdf, accessed September 9, 2013.

23. Wider Opportunities for Women, "WIA Reauthorization: What Local Workforce Boards Say About Services for Women," 2003, http://www.sixstrategies.org/files/local%20WIB%20survey%20factsheet (URL no longer active).

24. K. Shaw and S. Rab, "Market Rhetoric Versus Reality in Policy and Practice: The Workforce Investment Act and Access to Community College Education and Training," *Annals of the American Academy of Political and Social Science*, 586, 2003:172–193, at 192.

25. Ibid, 192.

26. Ibid, 192.

27. Women Work! "Congressional Testimony," July 11, 2007, http://www.womenwork.org/policy/WIArecommendations112408.pdf, accessed September 12, 2010 (URL no longer active).

28. K. Shaw, S. Goldrick-Rab, C. Mazzeo, and J. Jacobs, *Putting Poor People to Work: How the Work-First Idea Eroded College Access for the Poor* (New York: Russell Sage, 2006), 128.

29. M. Sosulski, *A Road to Inclusion: A Combined-Methods Analysis of Access to Post-Secondary Education for Women in the Illinois Public Aid System*, PhD dissertation, University of Wisconsin, Madison, 2004.

30. U.S. Department of Labor, "Bright Outlook Occupations, 2011," 2012, http://www.doleta.gov/performance/pfdocs/All_Bright_Outlook_Occupations2011.pdf, accessed September 9, 2013.

31. U.S. Department of Labor, "Charting Performance: Female Exiters by WIA Program PY 2008–2010," 2012, http://www.doleta.gov/performance/charts/Charting_Performance.cfm, accessed September 9, 2013.

32. Wider Opportunities for Women, "Reality Check: Promoting Self-Sufficiency in the Public Workforce System," 2006, http://www.wowonline.org/resources/publications/documents/WIBCurriculum-Script.pdf (URL no longer active).

33. Ibid.

34. Women Work! "Congressional Testimony."

35. M. Abramovitz, *Under Attack and Fighting Back: Women and Welfare in the United States* (New York: Monthly Review Press, 2000).

36. S. Gooden, "The Hidden Third Party: Welfare Recipients' Experiences with Employers," *Journal of Public Management and Social Policy* 5, 1999:59–83.

37. National Urban League, Institute for Opportunity and Equality, *Differences in TANF Support Services Utilization: Is There Adequate Monitoring to Ensure Program Quality?* (New York: National Urban League, 2002).

38. Women of Color Policy Network, "Gender, Race, Class and Welfare Reform," 2007, http://nychri.org/documents/WOCPNGenderRaceClass.pdf, accessed September 9, 2013.

39. A. Carnevale, T. Jayasundera, and B. Cheah, *The College Advantage: Weathering the Economic Storm*, Georgetown University, 2012, http://www9.georgetown.edu/grad/gppi/hpi/cew/pdfs/CollegeAdvantage.Full Report.081512.pdf, accessed September 9, 2013.

40. E. Sok, "Record Unemployment Among Older Workers Does Not Keep Them Out of the Job Market." U.S. Bureau of Labor Statistics, 2010, http://www.bls.gov/opub/ils/summary_10_04/older_workers.htm, accessed September 9, 2013.

Chapter 2

1. I. Lurie, *At the Front Lines of the Welfare System: A Perspective on the Decline in Welfare Caseloads* (New York: State University of New York Press, 2006), 2.

2. C. Kingsfisher, "How Providers Make Policy: An Analysis of Everyday Conversation in a Welfare Office." *Journal of Community & Applied Social Psychology* 8, 1998:119–136, at 119.

3. See Lurie, *At the Front Lines of the Welfare System*; M. C. Lennon and T. Corbett, *Policy into Action: Implementation Research and Welfare Reform* (Washington DC: Urban Institute Press, 2003); and M. K. Meyers, B. Glaser, and K. MacDonald, "On the Frontlines of Welfare Delivery: Are Workers Implementing Policy Reforms?" *Journal of Policy Analysis and Management* 17, 1998:1–22.

4. Good examples of this are found in Lurie, *At the Front Lines of the Welfare System*; J. Sandifort, A. Kalil, and J. Gottschalk, "The Mirror Has Two Faces: Welfare Clients and Front-Line Workers View Policy Reforms," *Journal of Poverty* 3, 1999:71–91; and E. Brodkin, "Policy Politics: If We Can't Govern, Can We Manage?" *Political Science Quarterly* 102, 1987:571–587.

5. Anne E. Casey Foundation, "The Unsolved Challenge of System Reform: The Condition of the Frontline Human Services Workforce," 2003, p. 12, http://www.aecf.org/KnowledgeCenter/Publications.aspx?pubguid=%7BA4B76C41 -76F0-4ACA-A475-1665F3519663%7D, accessed July 10, 2012.

6. For the ease of reading, I am referring to the workers in this chapter as "front-line workers."

7. The full state plans can be found at http://www.njsetc.net/njsetc/plan ning/unified (accessed September 9, 2013).

8. According to local officials in New Jersey, the salaries ranged from $38,000 to $50,000 annually.

9. U.S. Bureau of Labor Statistics, "Table 39: Median Weekly Earnings of Full-Time Wage and Salary Workers by Detailed Occupation and Sex," 2011, http://www.bls.gov/cps/cpsaat39.pdf, accessed September 9, 2013.

10. Public/Private Ventures, *Through a Kaleidoscope: How the Evolving Field of Workforce Development Impacts the Experiences of Frontline Workers in Three Cities*, Cornerstones for Kids, 2007, http://www.cps.ca.gov/workforceplanning/documents/07.11_Thru_Kaleid.pdf, accessed September 9, 2013.

11. Ibid.

12. R. W. Eberts, C. J. O'Leary, and K. J. DeRango, "A Frontline Decision Support System for One-Stop Centers," in R. W. Eberts, C. J. O'Leary, and S. A. Wandner (eds.), *Targeting Employment Services* (Kalamazoo, MI: W.E. Upjohn Institute for Employment Research, 2002).

13. U.S. Bureau of Labor Statistics, *Occupational Outlook Handbook: Social and Human Service Assistants*, 2010, http://www.bls.gov/ooh/community-and -social-service/social-and-human-service-assistants.htm, accessed September 9, 2013.

14. New Jersey State Employment and Training Commission, *New Jersey Unified Plan*, 2007, p. 141, http://njsetc.net.

15. Ibid, p. 142.

16. Ibid, p. 142.

17. Ibid, p. 142.

18. H. Hartmann, "Women, Recession and the Stimulus Package," *Dissent* 56, 2009:42–47.

19. See C. Figley, *Compassion Fatigue: Coping with Secondary Traumatic Stress Disorder in Those Who Treat the Traumatized* (New York: Brunner/Mazel, 1995); and B. H. Stamm, *Secondary Traumatic Stress: Self-Care Issues for Clinicians, Researchers and Educators*, 2nd ed. (Baltimore: Sidran Press, 1999).

20. Figley, *Compassion Fatigue*.

21. For more detail, see H. Bell, "Strengths and Secondary Trauma in Family Violence Work," *Social Work* 48, 2003:513–522; and H. Bell, S. Kulkarni, and L. Dalton, "Organizational Prevention of Vicarious Trauma," *Families in Society* 84, 2003:463–470.

22. For more detail, see T. Cornille and T. Meyers, "Secondary Traumatic Stress Among Child Protective Service Workers: Prevalence, Severity and Predictive Factors," *Traumatology* 5, 1999:15–31; B. Dane, "Child Welfare Workers: An Innovative Approach for Interacting with Secondary Trauma," *Jour-*

nal of Social Work Education 36, 2000:27–38; J. Pryce, K. Shackelford, and D. Pryce, *Secondary Traumatic Stress and the Child Welfare Professional* (Chicago: Lyceum Books, 2007); and C. Regehr, D. Hemsworth, B. Leslie, P. Howe, and S. Chau, "Predictors of Post-Traumatic Distress in Child Welfare Workers: A Linear Structural Equation Model," *Ontario Association of Children's Aid Societies Journal* 48, 2004:25–30.

23. For more detail, see D. Couper, "The Impact of the Sexually Abused Child's Pain on the Worker and the Team." *Journal of Social Work Practice* 14, 2000:9–16; and M. Cunningham, "The Impact of Sexual Abuse Treatment on the Social Work Clinician," *Child and Adolescent Social Work Journal* 16, 1999:277–290.

24. See K. Walsh-Burke, *Grief and Loss: Theories and Skills for Helping Professionals* (Boston: Pearson, 2006).

25. National Employment Law Project, *The Low Wage Recovery and Growing Inequality*, 2012, http://www.nelp.org/page/-/Job_Creation/LowWageRecovery 2012.pdf?nocdn=1, accessed September 9, 2013.

26. O. Sharone, "Constructing Unemployed Job Seekers as Professional Workers: The Depoliticizing Work-Game of Job Searching," *Qualitative Sociology* 30, 2011:403–416.

27. S. Morgen, "The Agency of Welfare Workers: Negotiating Devolution, Privatization, and the Meaning of Self-Sufficiency," *American Anthropologist* 103, 2001:747–761, at 752.

28. This need to encourage clients to settle for less in the labor market was borne out in research conducted by Szeltner, Van Horn, and Zukin, who in their survey of individuals who lost their jobs during the recession, learned that among those who did find new jobs, 49 percent reported that their job was a step down from the previous one they had held before, and 54 percent reported that the new job paid less than the one they had had before.

29. Morgen, "The Agency of Welfare Workers."

30. A. Hochschild, *The Managed Heart* (Berkeley: University of California Press, 1983).

31. This is somewhat similar to sociologist Lisa Dodson's finding of how workers engaged in "economic disobedience" to help address injustices they saw in the labor market or in public programs. For instance, she shares the example of a director of a child care center who misplaced paperwork so that children would not lose child care and parents would not lose jobs. L. Dodson, *The Moral Underground: How Ordinary Americans Subvert an Unfair Economy* (New York: The New Press, 2009). However, in my interviews, while the workers did not appear to engage in any type of economic disobedience, engaging in an act of kindness and framing it as something they could do to help the client is in a similar vein.

Chapter 3

1. H. Holtzer, "Workforce Development as an Antipoverty Strategy: What Do We Know? What Should We Do?" Working paper #08-17, National Poverty Center, Ann Arbor, Michigan, 2008.

2. Wider Opportunities for Women, "How Federal Job Training Programs Help Workers and the Economy; Attacks on Employment And Training Programs Are Arbitrary and Misdirected," written testimony submitted to Subcommittee on Higher Education and Workforce Training Committee on Education and the Workforce United States House of Representatives, 2011.

3. K. Shaw, S. Goldrick-Rab, C. Mazzeo, and J. Jacobs, *Putting Poor People to Work: How the Work-First Idea Eroded College Access for the Poor* (New York: Russell Sage, 2006).

4. C. J. O'Leary and R. W. Eberts, "The Wagner-Peyser Act and U.S. Employment Service: Seventy-Five Years of Matching Job Seekers and Employers," report prepared for the Center for Employment Security Education and Researchand the National Association of State Workforce Agencies, 2008.

5. N. Rose, "Gender, Race, and the Welfare State: Government Work Programs from the 1930s to the Present," *Feminist Studies* 19, 1993:319–342, at 324.

6. Shaw, Goldrick-Rab, Mazzeo, and Jacobs, *Putting Poor People to Work*, 22.

7. O'Leary and Eberts, "The Wagner-Peyser Act and U.S. Employment Service."

8. Ibid.

9. Shaw, Goldrick-Rab, Mazzeo, and Jacobs, *Putting Poor People to Work*, 22.

10. Ibid., 23.

11. W. N. Grubb and M. Lazerson, *The Education Gospel* (Cambridge, MA: Harvard University Press, 2004).

12. For a detailed description, see Shaw, Goldrick-Rab, Mazzeo, and Jacobs, *Putting Poor People to Work*, and M. Katz, *The Price of Citizenship: Redefining the American Welfare State* (New York: Metropolitan, 2001).

13. G. Lafer, *The Job Training Charade* (Ithaca, NY: Cornell University Press, 2002).

14. Shaw, Goldrick-Rab, Mazzeo, and Jacobs, *Putting Poor People to Work*.

15. Ibid, 24.

16. Ibid.

17. M. Gatta, *Not Just Getting By: The New Era of Flexible Workforce Development* (Lanham, MD: Lexington, 2005).

18. Shaw, Goldrick-Rab, Mazzeo, and Jacobs, *Putting Poor People to Work*, 100.

19. For a detailed description, see Shaw, Goldrick-Rab, Mazzeo, and Jacobs, *Putting Poor People to Work*.

20. Lafer, *The Job Training Charade*.

21. Shaw, Goldrick-Rab, Mazzeo, and Jacobs, *Putting Poor People to Work*, 25. See also Lafer, *The Job Training Charade*.

22. For a full report, see L. Weiss, "Opening Doors: How to Make the Workforce Investment Act Work for Women," Center for American Progress, 2010, http://www.americanprogress.org/issues/women/report/2010/07/01 /8165/opening-doors, accessed September 9, 2013.

23. A. Kessler-Harris, *In Pursuit of Equity: Women, Men and the Quest for Economic Citizenship in the 20th Century* (New York: Oxford University Press, 2001).

24. Ibid, 69.

25. G. Mink and R. Solinger, *Welfare: A Documentary History of Policy and Politics* (New York: New York University Press, 2003).

26. J. Grogger and L. Karoly, *Welfare Reform: Effects of a Decade of Change* (Cambridge, MA: Harvard University Press, 2005).

27. For a detailed discussion, see K. Luker, *Abortion and the Politics of Motherhood* (Berkeley, CA: University of California Press, 1985); and M. Abramovitz, *Under Attack and Fighting Back: Women and Welfare in the United States* (New York: Monthly Review Press, 2000).

28. Luker, *Abortion and the Politics of Motherhood*, 52.

29. The racial divide in regard to welfare policies cannot be understated. Sociologists Randy Albeda and Chris Tilly, among others, note that the Social Security Act perpetuated a racial double standard that continues to exist today. R. Albeda and C. Tilly, *Glass Ceilings and Bottomless Pits: Women's Work, Women's Poverty* (Boston: South End Press, 1997). The act's core programs—Unemployment Compensation and Old Age Assistance—excluded agricultural workers and domestic servants. These occupations were primarily occupied by black workers in the South.

30. Abramovitz, *Under Attack and Fighting Back*.

31. R. Solinger, "Dependency and Choice: The Two Faces of Eve," in Gwendolyn Mink (ed.), *Whose Welfare?* (Ithaca, NY: Cornell University Press, 1998).

32. F. Fox Piven and R. Cloward, *Regulating the Poor: The Functions of Public Welfare* (New York: Vintage Press, 1993), 129.

33. Ibid, 129.

34. Ibid, 134.

35. Ibid, 137. These data refer to individuals living in cities with populations of fifty thousand to five hundred thousand persons.

36. W. Stafford, D. Salas, and M. Mendex, *Gender, Race, Class and Welfare Reform* (New York: NYU Center for Leadership in Action, 2003).

37. Mink and Solinger, *Welfare*, 536.

Chapter 4

1. This directive came from the state Department of Labor and was a process they had been working on earlier.

2. It is important to stress that a new governor came into office in the time I began my research and conducted my follow-up focus groups. This led to changes at the top levels of the state Department of Labor, and they were working on the issues of customer service in the One Stops as a significant piece of reform throughout the state workforce system.

3. F. Ridzi, *Selling Welfare Reform: Work-First and the New Common Sense of Employment* (New York: New York University Press, 2009), 252.

4. H. J. Holtzer and R. I. Lerman, "The Future of Middle-Skill Jobs," Center on Children and Families, a report of the Brookings Institute, 2013, http://www.brookings.edu/~/media/research/files/papers/2009/2/middle%20 skill%20jobs%20holzer/02_middle_skill_jobs_holzer.pdf, accessed September 9, 2013.

5. National Employment Law Project, *The Low Wage Recovery and Growing Inequality*, 2012, http://www.nelp.org/page/-/Job_Creation/LowWageRecovery2012.pdf?nocdn=1, accessed September 9, 2013.

6. L. Mishel, "Entry Level Workers' Wages Fell in Lost Decade," 2012, http://www.epi.org/publication/ib327-young-workers-wages, accessed September 9, 2013.

7. Ibid.

8. U.S. Small Business Administration, Office of Advocacy, "Employer Firms, Establishments, Employment, and Annual Payroll Small Firm Size Classes, 2007," 2007, http://archive.sba.gov/advo/research/us_07ss.pdf, accessed September 9, 2013.

9. Wider Opportunities for Women, "The Economic Security Scorecard: Policy and Security in the States," 2013, http://www.wowonline.org/wp-content/uploads/2013/05/WOW-Economic-Security-Scorecard-2013.pdf, accessed September 9, 2013.

10. A. Berhardt, "The Future of Low-Wage Jobs: Case Studies in the Retail Industry," IEE Working Paper #10, 1999, 29.

11. M. Korczynski, "Service Work and Skills: An Overview," *Human Resource Management Journal* 15, 2005:1–12.

12. E. Appelbaum and J. Schmitt, "Low-Wage Work in High-Income Countries: Labor-Market Institutions and Business Strategy in the U.S. and Europe," *Human Relations* 62, 2009:1907–1934.

Index

Work Incentive (WIN), 103–104

Work Progress Administration (WPA), 103

Women: education and training opportunities and, 48–57; GI Bill and 103; intersections of race and class, 14; labor market experiences of, 13–14, 17–21, 48, 109, 115, 131; New Deal and, 102–103; New Jersey labor market, 23–24; nontraditional training of, 50–52, 96, 107–108, 119; recession and 15–16, 86–87; sex segregation, 16, 17–20, 48; welfare and 43–44, 46, 54, 57, 108–116; WIA and, 8, 28, 55–57

Women of Color Policy Network, 57

WomenWork!, 56